5

Jin Kobayashi

TRANSLATED AND ADAPTED BY
William Flanagan

LETTERED BY
Michaelis/Carpelis Design

BALLANTINE BOOKS • NEW YORK

School Rumble volume 5 is a work of fiction. Names, characters, places, and incidents are the products of the author's imagination or are used fictitiously. Any resemblance to actual events, locales, or persons, living or dead, is entirely coincidental.

A Del Rey Trade Paperback Original

Published in the United States by Del Rey Books, an imprint of The Random House Publishing Group, a division of Random House, Inc., New York.

DEL REY is a registered trademark and the Del Rey colophon is a trademark of Random House, Inc.

Publication rights arranged through Kodansha Ltd.

First published in Japan in 2004 by Kodansha Ltd., Tokyo

ISBN 978-0-345-49151-0

Printed in the United States of America

www.delreymanga.com

9 8 7 6 5 4 3 2

Translator and adaptor: William Flanagan
Lettering: Michaelis/Carpelis Design

Honorifics Explained

Throughout the Del Rey Manga books, you will find Japanese honorifics left intact in the translations. For those not familiar with how the Japanese use honorifics and, more important, how they differ from American honorifics, we present this brief overview.

Politeness has always been a critical facet of Japanese culture. Ever since the feudal era, when Japan was a highly stratified society, use of honorifics—which can be defined as polite speech that indicates relationship or status—has played an essential role in the Japanese language. When addressing someone in Japanese, an honorific usually takes the form of a suffix attached to one's name (example: "Asuna-san"), or as a title at the end of one's name or in place of the name itself (example: "Negi-sensei," or simply "Sensei!").

Honorifics can be expressions of respect or endearment. In the context of manga and anime, honorifics give insight into the nature of the relationship between characters. Many English translations leave out these important honorifics, and therefore distort the feel of the original Japanese. Because Japanese honorifics contain nuances that English honorifics lack, it is our policy at Del Rey not to translate them. Here, instead, is a guide to some of the honorifics you may encounter in Del Rey Manga.

-san: This is the most common honorific and is equivalent to Mr., Miss, Ms., or Mrs. It is the all-purpose honorific and can be used in any situation where politeness is required.

-sama: This is one level higher than "-san" and is used to confer great respect.

-dono: This comes from the word "tono," which means "lord." It is even a higher level than "-sama" and confers utmost respect.

-kun: This suffix is used at the end of boys' names to express familiarity or endearment. It is also sometimes used by men amongst friends, or when addressing someone younger or of a lower station.

-chan: This is used to express endearment, mostly toward girls. It is also used for little boys, pets, and even among lovers. It gives a sense of childish cuteness.

Bozu: This is an informal way to refer to a boy, similar to the English term "kid" or "squirt."

Sempai/Senpai: This title suggests that the addressee is one's senior in a group or organization. It is most often used in a school setting, where underclassmen refer to their upperclassmen as "sempai." It can also be used in the workplace, such as when a newer employee addresses an employee who has seniority in the company.

Kohai: This is the opposite of "—sempai" and is used toward underclassmen in school or newcomers in the workplace. It connotes that the addressee is of a lower station.

Sensei: Literally meaning "one who has come before," this title is used for teachers, doctors, or masters of any profession or art.

Onee-chan/Onii-chan: Older siblings are not commonly called by name but rather by the title "older sister" (*Onee-chan*) or "older brother" (*Onii-chan*). Depending on the relationship, *-san* or *-sama* can also be used instead of *-chan*. It can also be used with someone unrelated when the relationship resembles a sibling relationship.

[blank]: This is usually forgotten in these lists, but it is perhaps the most significant difference between Japanese and English. The lack of honorific means that the speaker has permission to address the person in a very intimate way. Usually, only family, spouses, or very close friends have this kind of permission. Known as yobisute, it can be gratifying when someone who has earned the intimacy starts to call one by one's name without an honorific. But when that intimacy hasn't been earned, it can be very insulting.

Cultural Note

To preserve some of the humor found in *School Rumble*, we have elected to keep Japanese names in their original Japanese order—that is to say, with the family name first, followed by the personal name. So when you hear the name Tsukamoto Tenma, Tenma is just one member of the Tsukamoto family.

School Rumble 5
Jin Kobayashi

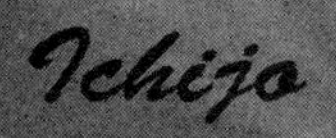
Ichijo

Contents

Sasakura

あらすじ　*Story*

Tsukamoto Tenma is in the second year of high school. She is our heroine. And like many, many girls her age, she is in love. However, she can't seem to make her feelings known to Karasuma Ôji, her classmate and the man she loves. And that's pretty much the way that *School Rumble* Volume 5 begins. A guy with a beard gets into fights and draws manga. Girls wear masks and crush apples with their bare hands...and with that, our story really begins to heat up! Even so, it's still a romantic comedy.

登場人物　*Characters*

I'M HERE!
CHATTER
CHATTER
AH HA HA!
#59 GROUNDHOG DAY
WHAT? BUT YOU SEE, ABOUT THAT...
ON DUTY: IMADORI, ICHIJÔ
BY THE WAY, ERI-CHAN, WHAT DO YOU THINK OF BEARDS?
CHATTER
CHATTER
WELL... IT DEPENDS ON WHO'S WEARING IT. SOME LOOK GREAT AND SOME ARE JUST AWFUL!
WHAT ABOUT LAZY BEARDS?
LAZY BEARDS?
WHAT'S THAT?
MANGOKU, OF COURSE! MANGOKU!
HIS IS SO COOL!
UM... TSUKAMOTO-SAN?
EH?
AH!
SHE ISN'T WEARING HER BRAID TODAY.
HAVE YOU SEEN IMADORI? WE'RE ON DUTY AND HAVE WORK...
I WARNED HIM ABOUT IT BUT...
HUH? DIDN'T YOU SEE HIM IN THE HALLWAY?
I SAW HIM CHATTING WITH MIHARA AND THOSE GIRLS.
GOOD WORK!
REALLY? THANKS!
I FEEL SORRY FOR YOU.
BEING TEAMED WITH THAT IDIOT.
I'M NOT WORRIED ABOUT THAT.
SEE YOU!
TMP
SHE'S NOT A BAD KID. I NEVER TALKED TO HER MUCH, BUT...
THAT'S WHAT WORRIES ME.
IT IS IMADORI, AFTER ALL.

THEN HOW ABOUT THIS SUNDAY?
I CAN'T SWIM, BUT THAT BEACH IS A REALLY NICE PLACE.
THERE ARE EVEN DESERTED ISLANDS.
EH? BUT DIDN'T YOU ALREADY GO THERE FOR SUMMER VACATION WITH SUÔ AND THAT GROUP?
DON'T BE DUMB! THE LAST TRIP *HAS* TO BE WITH YOU GUYS!
THERE HE IS, BUT SHOULD I SAY ANYTHING?
I'M BAD AT BARGING IN.
すっ SST
!
POP
HEY, IMADORI!!
YESSS! MIKO-CHIN?!
WHAT? WHAT? WHAT?
TWRL
I GET IT! YOU'RE WORRIED BECAUSE I'M TALKING TO OTHER GIRLS, RIGHT?
I GOT IT, RIGHT?
FOOL!
IT'S ICHIJÔ!
YOU'RE ON DUTY WITH HER!
TH-THANK YOU, SUÔ-SAN...
UM... I'M SORRY TO INTERRUPT YOUR CONVER-SATION...
ACTUALLY... IMADORI-KUN, YOU AND I ARE ON DUTY TOGETHER TODAY...
AND THAT'S WHY...
HERE!
TAKE HIM AWAY.
BWIMP
TH-THANK...
...YOU.
......

AWWW! THIS IS SUCH A PAIN!
I HATE BEING ON DUTY!
GET SOMEBODY ELSE TO DO IT!
MUMBLE MUMBLE
KARAK
GRUMBLE GRUMBLE
IT'S OUR JOB.
DO YOU REALLY NEED ME AROUND?
YOU CAN CARRY THEM ALONE!
AH!
THIS IS IT! LET'S GATHER THIS WOOD UP!
UMPH! THIS IS PRETTY HEAVY! I CAN'T CARRY THESE ALONE!
ZUMPH
WHAT?
WHOOSH
TWRL
LISTEN... YOU REALLY SHOULD BE DOING THIS ALONE, ICHI-SAN.
EH?! I-I COULDN'T!
IT'D BE IMPOSSIBLE!
BUT YOU'RE ICHI-SAN, RIGHT?
RUNNING AT 10 MILLION HORSEPOWER?
NO! NEVER!!
J-JUST HELP OUT LIKE YOU'RE SUPPOSED TO!
AND STOP CALLING ME ICHI-SAN!

....
I-I'M SORRY. ...... YELLING LIKE THAT...
AH! UM... DID YOU...GO OFF TO THE BEACH?
YEAH...WITH MIKO-CHIN, HER FRIENDS, AND SOME STUPID GUYS. HOW ABOUT YOU?
ME?
I THINK IT WOULD'VE BEEN NICE TO GO. I ENVY YOU.
IT COULDN'T BE THAT IMADORI-KUN FORGOT HIS PROMISE TO TAKE ME ON A DATE, COULD IT?
I CAN TAKE MY HANDS OFF THIS, AND SHE DOESN'T EVEN NOTICE
SEE?
WHAT DID YOU DO FOR SUMMER VACATION?
EH? OH, RIGHT! MOSTLY PUSHUPS, STRENGTH TRAINING ON MY BACK AND ABS.
AND ASIDE FROM THAT...
I DID SOME SPRINTING, AND I STEPPED UP MY MORNING AND EVENING WORK-OUTS...
...AND... ...... BUT THAT'S REALLY NOTHING...
ZUUUUN
TREMBLE TREMBLE
HEY, THIS IS HEAVY!!
COME ON, JUST GRAB A HOLD OF THESE THINGS!

Ichijô: A Veteran of Amateur Wrestling.

YEAH, BUT...
YOU HAD AT LEAST ONE DATE, RIGHT?
EH?
I... UM...
TH-THERE WAS A... PROMISE FOR A DATE...
FROM... ...YOU...
OH, MAN, AM I HUNGRY!
AND MY ARMS ARE TREMBLING ALL OVER!
SIGH
HASN'T BEEN LISTEN-ING.
HE DID FORGET, HUH?
CRESTFALLEN
ONE PLUS ONE IS TWO. TWO PLUS TWO IS FOUR.
WE NEED THE COURAGE OF ALL OF YOU!
GO! NO. 1!! FLY! NO. 2!!
I WANTED TO...GO ON A DATE...
SIGH
DATE?!
TWIK
DATE?!
ZHATT
EH?!
THEN I'LL TAKE YOU...
HA! HA! HA! HATENKÔ~! HATENKÔ ROBO! DOJIBIRON~!
I ALMOST HAVE THE FEELING THAT SOMETHING LIKE THIS MIGHT HAVE HAPPENED BEFORE...
I-IS THIS DÉJÀ VU?!
BUT WHY? SHE CERTAINLY ISN'T D IN ANY WAY, SHAPE OR FORM. WHY WOULD I EVER ASK HER OUT?

YOU GOT THAT RIGHT!
I'VE GOT SO MUCH THAT I COULD EVEN ASK...
...ICHIJÔ OUT ON A DATE!
AH!
OKAY, I'LL GO.
BULUUM BULUUM
ボワン ボワン
OH! NOW I REMEMBER!! WHEN I GOT PAID, I WAS SO HAPPY I UNWITTINGLY ASKED ICHIJÔ...
...OUT ON A DATE!!
I FORGOT ALL ABOUT IT! OH, YEAH. SO THAT'S WHY SHE'S BEEN GOING ON ABOUT DATES. A DATE...A DATE, HUH...?
SO THE WHOLE REASON SHE FORCED ME TO WORK ON DUTY WAS TO BRING THIS UP?!
THAT MEANS...
THAT I'M...
...ABOUT TO BE EATEN...
...IN A FEW MINUTES?!
O-OH, NO! IF WE KEEP TALKING ABOUT DATES...WILL I BECOME A VICTIM OF THIS SUPER-STRONG SPACE-ALIEN WOMAN? OR RATHER, THIS PREDATOR?
GRAAAH
GRNNN
TRMBL TRMBLE
IMADORI EYE!
RIGHT! FROM HERE ON OUT, I MUST NEVER BRING UP THE WORD DATE!
I'LL TAKE THE INITIATIVE AND NEVER BRING UP DATES!
FLASH
GO, KYÔSUKE! YOU CAN DO IT!!
HEY, MIKO-CHIN, LET'S GO ON A DATE TOGETHER!
TWIRL
くるっ
NEVER, YOU ABSOLUTE FOOL.
STP STP
スタ スタ
Call Him Pavlov's Boy.
......!
......
は〜
PHEW...
THAT WAS CLOSE! I DON'T THINK SHE HEARD!

Imadori Implodes; Ichijô Wins by Default.

59· · · · · · · · ·Fin

School
Rumble

60 TRADING PLACES
KACHANG
RATTLE
YOU'RE GETTING INTO YOUR WORKOUT, HUH, ICHIJÔ?
YES, SIR!
TODAY, I HAVE TO DO TWO DAYS' WORTH OF WORKOUT!
OH! SO YOU'VE ALREADY FIGURED IT OUT?
YOU SEE, WE JUST GOT CHALLENGED TO A MATCH.
HAPPENED SO SUDDENLY.
THEY'VE EVEN GOT FOREIGN STUDENTS. THEY'RE A POWERFUL SCHOOL!!
KLANNG
EH?
YOU MEAN FOR TOMORROW?

2-C
CHATTER
わい わい
CHATTER
おおっ
WHOA
ホーラ
SEE?
THEY'RE PICTURES FROM CAMP!!
HEEY!
W-WOW! LOOK AT THE LOVERS!!
HANAI, DON'T YOU LOOK A LITTLE BLURRED AROUND YOUR FACE?
THAT... ISN'T MY HAND THERE.
IT DOESN'T EVEN LOOK SIMILAR.
EH?!
SO HOW'D THAT HAPPEN, ANYWAY?
THIS IS WEIRD TOO. LOOK AT THAT AURA!
WELL, TO TELL THE TRUTH...
SAY NOTHING!!!
L-LOOK! COULD IT BE THAT YAKUMO-CHAN HAS GONE BEYOND C TO...
IMADORI, YOU CRETIN!!
THAT'S A GOOD QUESTION!
HA!! YOU'LL NEVER KNOW!!
.....
.....
BUT NOTHING BEATS MIKO-CHIN! WHY? BECAUSE SHE'S... D!!
YOU... PERVERTED...
GAKAAN
EH?
NO. I THINK MIKO-CHAN'S SIZE IS...
!!
N-NO, I'M NOT!!
WHAT ARE YOU SAYING?!
SHT
GLANCE
!!
.....
STARE
MUMBLE MUMBLE
I-I SEE IT NOW!
I MUST HAVE UNDER-ESTIMATED!
I SHOULD TAKE MORE CARE!
IMADORI-KUN, YOU SHOULD STOP CONCENTRATING ONLY ON GIRLS' CHESTS.
YOU'RE A BAD, BAD BOY.
THERE, THERE, TENMA-CHAN. YOU STILL HAVE LOTS OF TIME!
DON'T BE DISCOURAGED.
YOU WANNA GET BITTEN?!
ぽむ!
POFF
PI

NOW THAT I THINK OF IT...
WHERE'S HARIMA-KUN?
HE HASN'T BEEN BACK FOR A WHILE.
ON THE ROOF, PROBABLY.
HE'S BEEN GROWING OUT HIS BEARD LATELY.
I DON'T KNOW WHAT BROUGHT IT ON...
AH! YOU NOTICED THAT, TOO?!
KIND OF LIKE LINCOLN.
WHAT ARE YOU GUYS TALKING ABOUT?
OKAY, I'LL GO LOOK FOR HIM!
TMP
RIGHT!
GOOD IDEA
WHUMP
AH!
I-I'M SORRY!
KARERIN! NO, I'M SORRY!
WHAT'S WRONG?
EH?
AH! NO PROBLEM... I-IS IMADORI HERE?
AND THAT NICKNAME ISN'T...
BUSTLE
BUSTLE
EH?
IMADORI'S IN THE CLASSROOM.
ARE YOU TWO ON DUTY?
I'LL GO CALL HIM.

IMAD–
MRFLF!!
ずるずる
ZGGL
ZGGL
MRF?!
URM?!
URM?!
SORRY, BUT UM... UH...THE TRUTH IS...
EHHH?!
THAT REALLY HAPPENED? YOU MEAN YOU AND IMAD–
SHH! SHH!
ぎゅううっ
GWMMMM
G-G-GAN'D BREAVE!
AH! S-SORRY...
カッキ
KRAK
BUT... ACTUALLY, AN EXHIBITION MATCH WAS SUDDENLY SCHEDULED...
AND SO...I CAN'T GO ON THE DATE...
SO I NEED TO TELL IMADORI-KUN ABOUT IT...
NEVER!!
EH?
.....
ぽんっ
PONN
?
THINK ABOUT IT, KARERIN! HOW MANY MATCHES HAVE YOU HAD THIS SUMMER?
EH? U-UM...25, MAYBE?
AND LET'S NOT DO THE KARERIN.
OKAY...
Karerin = Ichi-san = Ichijô Karen.

A Master at Pushing Others into Relationships.

AND DATES?!
WHOOSH
EH?
HOW MANY DATES?
EHH... UMM...
ONE TIME...
MAYBE LESS...
THEN IT'S DECIDED!!
YOU CAN HAVE THOSE OLD MATCHES ANYTIME!
JUST LEAVE EVERYTHING TO ME!
DOOOOM
SOMETHING AKIN TO ONEE-CHAN POWER TURNING ON.
EH?
I'LL HANDLE THE DETAILS. YOU, KARERIN, JUST GO ON YOUR DATE, AND DON'T WORRY ABOUT A THING!
RIGHT?
.....
!!
TH—
THANK YOU!
AND FORGET THE KARERIN NICKNAME, OKAY?
MEEEN
MEEEN
MEEEN
KEEEE
SHHHH
BEEP BEEP
GRRRMM
MEEEN MEEEN
IMADORI-KUN... IS LATE, HUH...
BUT WHAT AM I SUPPOSED TO SAY WHEN HE GETS HERE?
SHOULD I SAY THAT I JUST GOT HERE TOO?
CHATTER
CHATTER

HEY CUTIE, WANNA GO FOR A DRINK?
I SHOULD PROBABLY PRACTICE...
I-I JUST GOT HERE, TOO.
I JUST GOT HERE, TOO...
MUMBLE MUMBLE
ALREADY FORGOTTEN THE REASON HE CAME HERE.
WHO ARE YOU? GO AWAY!!
AW, THAT'S TOO BAD!
GOOD BYE.
HEY... ♡
POFF
SEE YOUR BOYFRIEND LATER!
FIRST COME HAVE A DRINK WITH ME!
EH?
GLEEM
GLEEM
TWRL
EH?
AH!
UM...
I-I JUST GOT HERE...
TOO!!
GAMPH
I-I'M SORRY! YOU TOLD A JOKE AND I DIDN'T LAUGH AT ALL...
.....
EH? OH! AH, HA, HA!
DON'T WORRY ABOUT IT!!
JUST ABOUT THEN, AT THE MATCH...
ESCAPED DEATH BY THE SKIN OF MY TEETH, HUH?
HUH?

Duwa!!

DUWA!!
MUSCLE
SHF
PA-KLINK
......
...... THIS MIGHT BE ROUGH!
FIP
AN EXCHANGE STUDENT FROM MEXICO.
THUNK
JUWA!!
(WHERE'S THE ROPE? WHERE'S THE ROPE?)
STRUGGLE
STRUGGLE
NEE-SAN... THIS ISN'T... ...THAT KIND OF WRESTLING...
FORCED TO COME ALONG AS TENMA'S SECOND.

60 . . . . Fin

I-IMADORI-KUN, WHAT SPORTS ARE YOU GOOD AT?
NONE OF 'EM.
TH-THEN MARTIAL ARTS OR SOME-THING LIKE THAT...
I HATE 'EM ALL.
I DON'T DO IDIOTIC STUFF LIKE THAT.
61 A STAR IS BORN
BUT YOU HAVE GOOD REFLEXES, HUH?
YEAH.
ICHIJÔ IS PANICKING BECAUSE SHE CAN'T KEEP THE CONVER-SATION GOING.
WH-WHAT'LL I DO? I'VE GOT NOTHING TO TALK ABOUT.
IMADORI KNOWS THAT, HE JUST DOESN'T CARE.
IF I KEEP THINGS BORING, IT CAN END HERE.
I-I KNOW! I'LL USE THAT!
I'LL OPEN ONE OF THE BAGS THAT TSUKAMOTO-SAN GAVE ME!
ZZZZZZIP
YOU DON'T KNOW HOW TO DATE, RIGHT?
WELL, THIS MAY HELP...
WHAT IS IT?
HEH HEH HEH!
A BAG WITH ALL THE SECRETS OF A GOOD DATE!
IF YOUR DATE IS IN DANGER, THEN OPEN THE BAG.
THERE ARE THREE WITHIN!
TH-THANK YOU, TSUKAMOTO-SAN!
BUT WHAT'S WITH THE CLOTHES?
THINK NOTHING OF IT. I AM AN ALLY TO ALL GIRLS WHO WISH TO CHANGE.
THAT WITHIN THE BAG IS CERTAIN TO RESCUE YOU IN YOUR DATE'S TIME OF NEED!
SO WHAT'S INSIDE IT?
MAYBE A BOOK WITH ALL SORTS OF SUBJECTS OF CONVERSA-TION? OKAY, TSUKAMOTO-SAN, I'M OPEN-ING IT!
ZLIPP
NO. 1

No Instruction Booklet.
WHAT AM I SUPPOSED TO DO WITH THIS? EAT IT?
T-TSUKAMOTO-SAN, I DON'T UNDERSTAND!
.....
...GIMME!
GRATCH
かしっ
EH?
LOOK AT ME! I'M SOO BIG!
D! D!
WOW!
KLAP KLAP
ぱち ぱち
BWOOMBA
BWOOMBA
APPLE INSIDE THERE.
HA HA HA HA HA HA HA HA HA HA HA...
IDIOT!
THERE'S NO MALICE IN IT.
BWOOMBA BWOOMBA
くる TWIRL
くる TWIRL
I'M NOT QUITE SURE WHY...
BUT IMADORI-KUN IS HAVING SO MUCH FUN!
THANK YOU, TSUKAMOTO-SAN!
GREAT AMOUNTS OF TOLERANCE.

Imadori: Actually He Loves Special Effects Films and Anime.

THERE IS SOME-BODY WHO THINKS ONLY OF YOU...
...AND IS ALWAYS BESIDE YOU!!
HYAA!
WHOA!!
GRAAH!
HAYAAH!
GAWHOOM
YEAH!!
IT WAS SO DARK...
...THEY COULDN'T SEE EACH OTHER'S FACES.
MOMMY, WHAT'S THAT?
BAMBAMBAMBAM
KA-KLANNG
KRANNCH
BUT IT WAS AS IF THE TWO WERE DRAWN CLOSELY TOGETHER.
EVERY-BODY, LET'S GO!!
YEAH!
"THIS IS TRULY WHAT A DATE IS," ICHIJÔ THOUGHT. AND SHE WAS THE ONLY ONE IN THE THEATER TO THINK THAT.
WHOA!
OH, THAT WAS SO COOL!!
REALLY, ONLY A MOVIE CAN MAKE A GUY FEEL SATISFIED!
DID YOU SEE IT? WHEN THEY DID THE HATENKÔ-CHOP?!
VWAKK
AH!
THWIM
......

YOU'VE GOT A LOTTA GUTS!!
YOU REALLY HAVE A DEATH WISH, HUH?
SH-SHUT UP!!
IT'S YOUR OWN FAULT FOR COMING UP SO CLOSE!
IMADORI-SAN!!
STRUGGLE STRUGGLE
I HAVE TO SAVE IMADORI-SAN! B-BUT...
I-I DON'T WANT PEOPLE TO SAY THAT I'M A VIOLENT WOMAN! WHAT'LL I DO?
I KNOW! THAT LAST BAG!
PLEASE! HELP ME OUT!!
NEED SOME GUIDANCE!!
SLIP
TH-THIS IS...
I GET IT! THAT'S WHAT THIS IS ALL ABOUT!!
S-STOP RIGHT THERE!!
HM?!

R-RELEASE THAT MAN RIGHT NOW!!
HAS A MASK ON.
MUSCLE
APPLE.
CHARACTER: DOJIBIRON
WHA-?!!
GRAAH
WHAT THE HELL IS THIS?!
ARE YOU SAYING I GOTTA STOP OR YOU'LL HURT THAT APPLE?! THERE ARE LIMITS TO THE CRAP I'LL TAKE-
GRUNNCH
MUSCLE
KRICH KRICH
..... PLEASE FORGIVE ME.
PLIP PLIP
..... WH-WHO ARE YOU?
DOJIBIRON?
MUSCLE
SST
HM?

We Dub Her Dojibiron Pink!

61 . . . . Fin

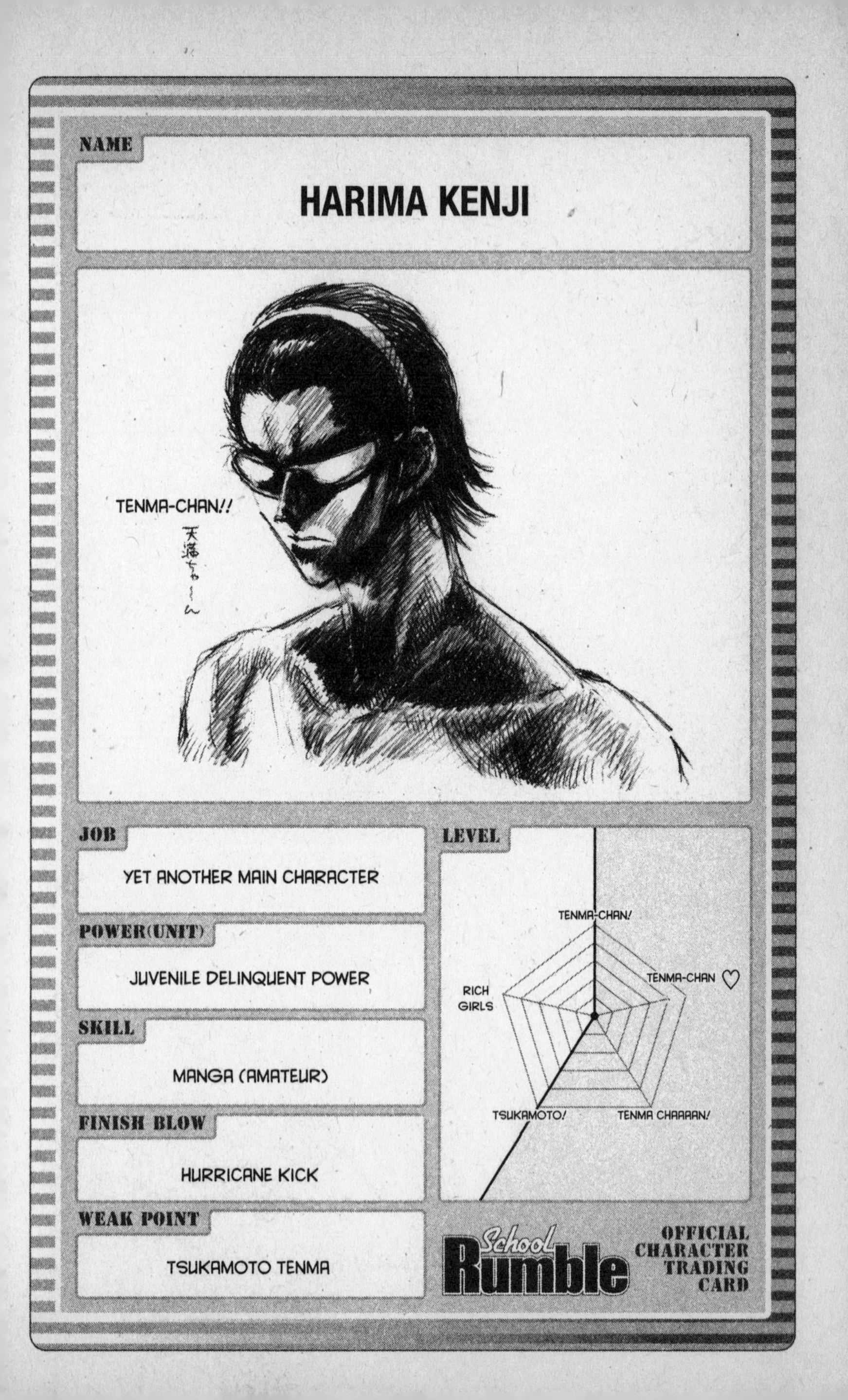
NAME
HARIMA KENJI
TENMA-CHAN!!
天満ちゃ～ん
JOB
YET ANOTHER MAIN CHARACTER
POWER(UNIT)
JUVENILE DELINQUENT POWER
SKILL
MANGA (AMATEUR)
FINISH BLOW
HURRICANE KICK
WEAK POINT
TSUKAMOTO TENMA
LEVEL
TENMA-CHAN!
TENMA-CHAN ♡
RICH GIRLS
TSUKAMOTO!
TENMA CHAAAAN!
School Rumble
OFFICIAL CHARACTER TRADING CARD

A VIRTUAL WEDDING?
YES! WE'RE USING IT FOR PUBLICITY.
WE DO A MAKE-BELIEVE WEDDING, TAKE PICTURES, AND USE THEM IN A PAMPHLET.
AND...
YOU WANT ME TO PLAY THE BRIDE?
YOU FIT THE IMAGE TO A TEE!
WHEE
WHEE
IF IT'S YOU, YAKUMO, ANYBODY WOULD BELIEVE IT!
FX TK?
JUUUN JAAAN JUUUN
YAKUMO-NEE-CHAN! YOU'RE GETTING MARRIED?
WOW!
I WANNA SEE THAT! NEE-CHAN IN A WEDDING DRESS?
SEE?
MAYBE, BUT, UM...
DO IT!
I KNOW!
YOU'RE WORRIED OVER WHO WILL PLAY THE GROOM. RIGHT?
......
DON'T GIVE IT A THOUGHT!
THERE'S A PERFECT GUY AT MY PART-TIME JOB.
I'M GOING TO ASK HIM, SO YOU CAN RELAX.
62 THE GRADUATE

ON THE DAY...
YAKUMO-KUN!!
UM...
I'M SORRY, YAKUMO...
THE GUY AT WORK COULDN'T MAKE IT.
AND THEN HANAI-SEMPAI...
.....
SO SHOULD WE CALL THIS OFF?
UM... .....
I REALLY DID WANT TO SEE WHAT YOU'D LOOK LIKE AS A BRIDE, BUT...
N-NO... IT'S OKAY...
I GUESS...
THANK YOU!!
AND SORRY!
A SERIOUS FACE?
SHNT
YOU MEAN LIKE THIS?
AHH!
THAT'S REALLY A GREAT LOOK!
AND IF YOU STAY SILENT, YOU'LL LOOK EVEN BETTER!
THAT ISN'T PRAISE, SARAH-KUN! HA, HA, HA!
PI
PI
PI
....

Chinese Restaurant
I HEARD IT ALL, ASÔ!!
YOU TURNED DOWN THE GROOM'S POSITION?!
YOU GOTTA BE KIDDING!
WHERE'D YOU HEAR ABOUT THAT?
FUYUKI TOLD ME.
SEE?
HE'S THE BEST WHEN YOU WANT INFO.
I HAVE ERRANDS AFTER WORK.
A PREVIOUS ENGAGEMENT.
WHO CARES ABOUT ERRANDS?!
YOU HAD THE CHANCE TO GET INTO A TWO-SHOT WITH TSUKAMOTO!
WERE YOU RAISED BY WOLVES OR SOMETHING?
YOU IDIOT!
WHATEVER. HURRY UP AND ORDER.
WE'RE RUNNING A BUSINESS HERE.
HERE'S THE OOLONG TEA YOU ORDERED.
TONK
BUT THIS IS WITH TSUKAMOTO!
UNDERSTAND?!
HUH?
NO, I MUST DEFEAT MY ENEMY BEFORE I DRINK.
I HEARD THAT THEY DECIDED THAT HANAI WOULD STAND WITH TSUKAMOTO.
YOU HEARD ABOUT THAT?
DON'T KNOW. DON'T CARE.
KATAK
TAK
TAK
M-MISTER? MISTER?
I WISH I WERE HIM!!!
KATAK
WHOOM
GRMP
DORRRMM

GRMM
GRMM
GRMM
I WILL NEVER ALLOW THIS!
NO BEARDLESS WIMP HAS THE RIGHT TO STAND NEXT TO THE BRIDE TSUKAMOTO TENMA! THE GROOM...
...MUST BE ME!!
Aww, It's You?
SST...
KLUNK

わあああ…!!
WAAAAA!
ぉーっ
WHOA!
YOU'RE SO PRETTY!!
NEE-CHAN! YOU'RE REALLY CUTE!
WHEE-WOO!
HEY! YOU KIDS ARE THE CHOIR! SING!
..... SH—
SHE'S BEAU-TIFUL!

YAKUMO-KUN...
THIS IS ALMOST LIKE A DREAM...
BWAAN
I THINK THE GUY'S CRYING!
YOU PROBABLY DON'T REALIZE MY FEELINGS...
...BUT NOW, I CAN SAY IT!!
A-ACTUALLY, I'VE ALWAYS...
WHAAAAMM
THIS CEREMONY STOPS RIGHT NOW!!!
EH...?
WH... WHO'S THERE?!

Hanai Haruki: In Complete Confusion.

KAGRASSH
GAH!!
SHT
TAK
GRIMP
?!

There Are Feathers Flying.

62· · · · · · · · ·Fin

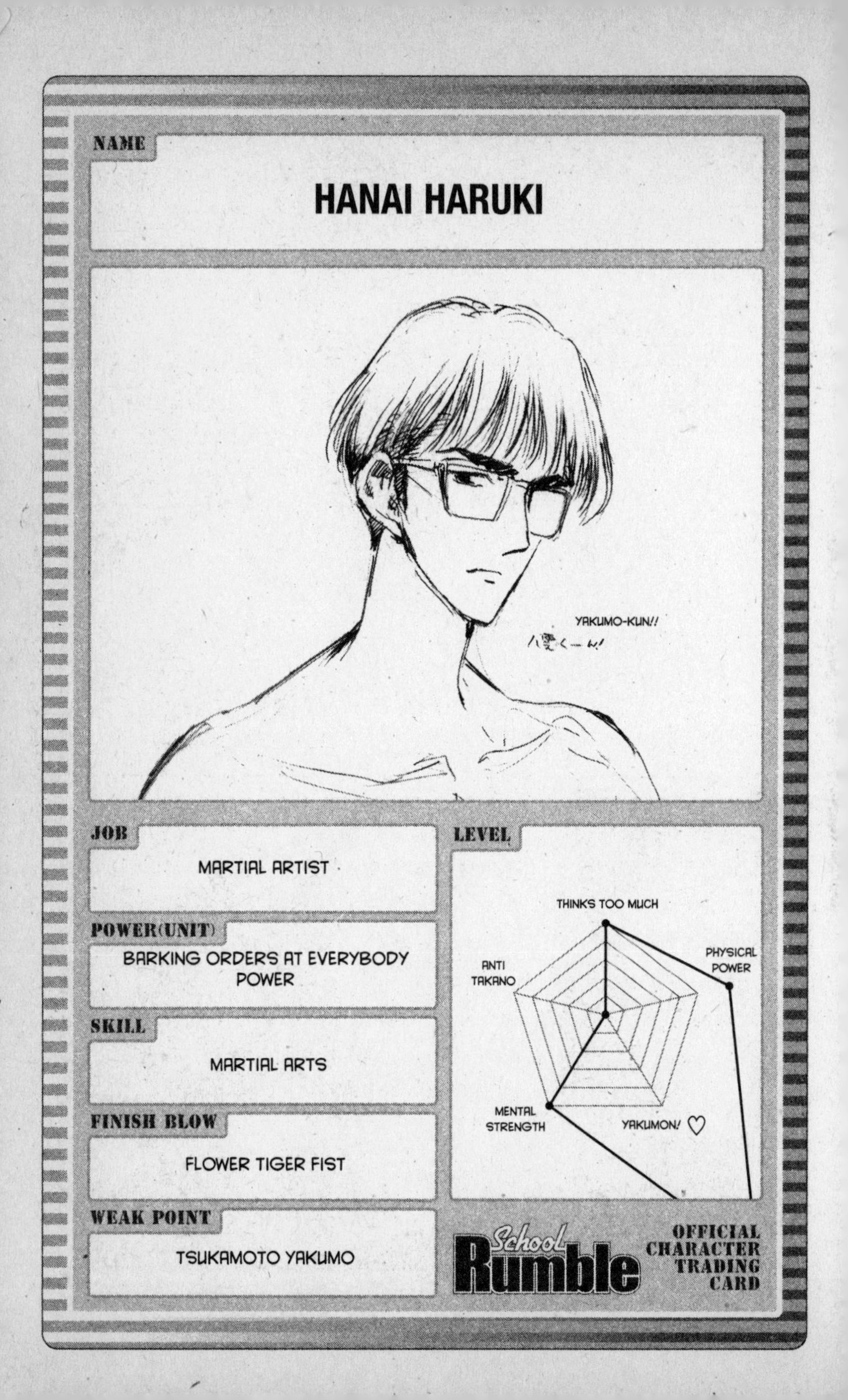
NAME
HANAI HARUKI
YAKUMO-KUN!!
八雲く〜ん!
JOB
MARTIAL ARTIST
POWER(UNIT)
BARKING ORDERS AT EVERYBODY POWER
SKILL
MARTIAL ARTS
FINISH BLOW
FLOWER TIGER FIST
WEAK POINT
TSUKAMOTO YAKUMO
LEVEL
THINKS TOO MUCH
PHYSICAL POWER
ANTI TAKANO
MENTAL STRENGTH
YAKUMON! ♡
School Rumble
OFFICIAL CHARACTER TRADING CARD

FLUTTER
Humans Attract Each Other...Humans Hate Each Other...All in the Name of Love.
63 LOVER COME BACK
WHAT'S THE MEANING OF THIS, HARIMA...?
GATCH
VWIM VWIM VWIM
YOU WILL NOW HAND TSUKAMOTO-KUN OVER TO ME!!

I'VE RECAST YOUR PART. SORRY, BUT FIND ANOTHER WOMAN.
.... UM...
STILL HASN'T NOTICED.
CHATTER
OH, MY!
THAT'S ADVICE I CAN'T ACCEPT!
SHE IS THE WORLD'S MOST WONDERFUL WOMAN, AND NO OTHERS MATCH HER.
CHATTER WHAT? WHAT?
IT'S GOTTA BE HER OLD BOY-FRIEND HERE TO STEAL THE BRIDE!
WHAT'S GONNA HAPPEN?
THIS IS GREAT! WHO CARES WHY, JUST START FIGHTING!
....
IT SEEMS YOU DO UNDER-STAND.
DIDN'T EXPECT THAT FROM A GUY IN GLASSES.
!
YOU'RE EXACTLY RIGHT.
FWUFF
WAIT FOR A FEW MOMENTS.
....
STILL HASN'T NOTICED.
GMP
THEN I'LL USE EASIER WORDS.
YOU'RE JUST NOT GOOD ENOUGH FOR THE PART!!
WHFF
SLUUM
LEAVE!!
TMP

ZAZAZAZAAA
HA!
HA!
HA!
WHOA!!!
I HAVE YOU NOW!!
GWAA
GAH!!
TSK!
GRIMP
GRANCH
THWAKAMM
NGAA!!
ROLLROLLROLL
GRIK
URRN...

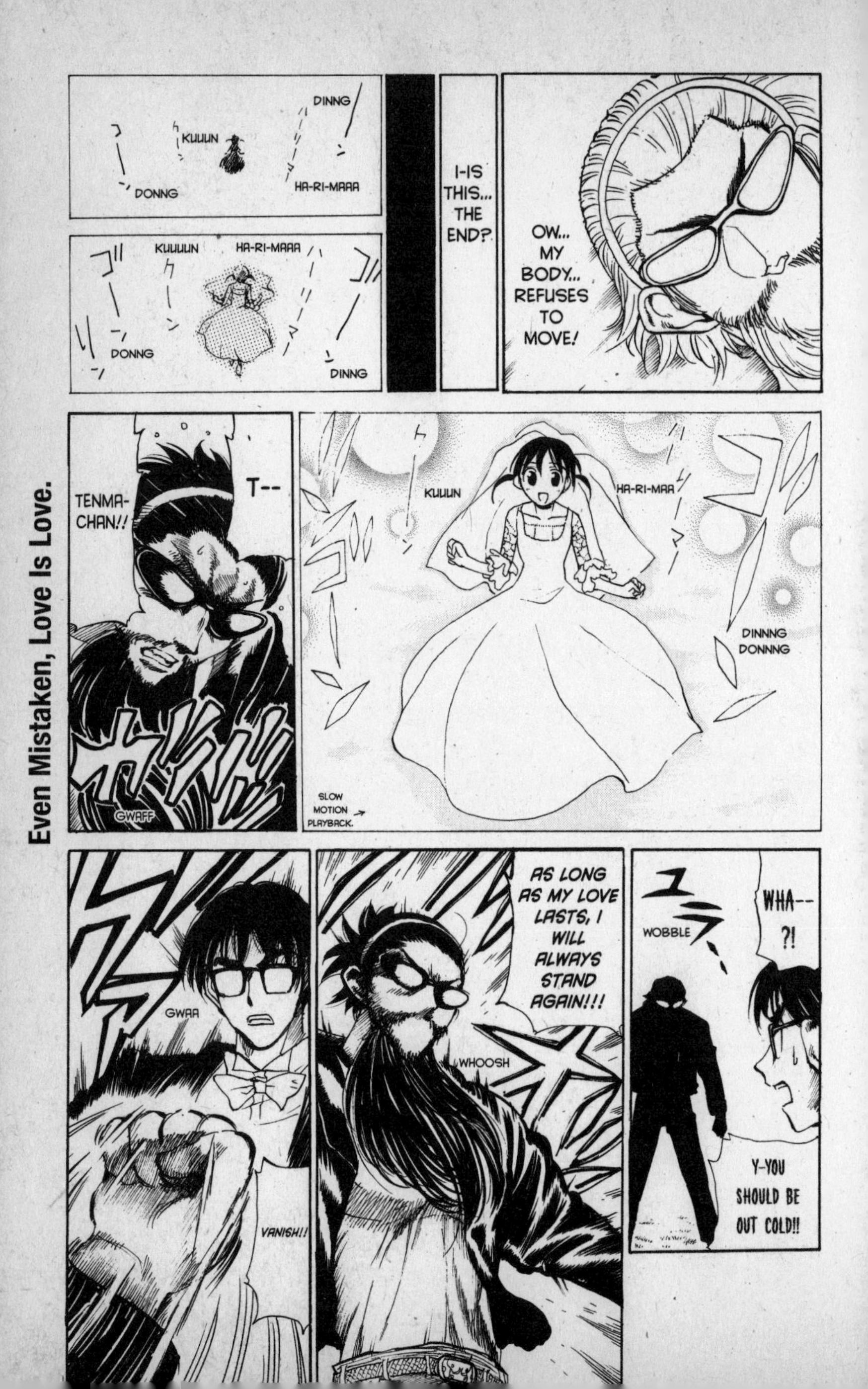
OW... MY BODY... REFUSES TO MOVE!
I-IS THIS... THE END?
DINNG
KUUUN
HA-RI-MAAA
DONNG
KUUUUN
HA-RI-MAAA
DONNG
DINNG
KUUUN
HA-RI-MAA
DINNNG DONNNG
SLOW MOTION PLAYBACK.
T--
TENMA-CHAN!!
GWAFF
WHA--?!
WOBBLE
Y-YOU SHOULD BE OUT COLD!!
AS LONG AS MY LOVE LASTS, I WILL ALWAYS STAND AGAIN!!!
WHOOSH
GWAA
VANISH!!

DOWOON
DACHAM
GWAAH!
I'M... LOSING... CONSCIOUSNESS!
WHERE WAS HE ABLE TO FIND THAT POWER...? HAVE...I LOST?
...CHIIII...
HA-NA-IIII...
...IIII CHIII... DONNG
DINNNG DONNNG
DINNG DONNG
YEAH, THIS IS IN SLOW MOTION PLAYBACK TOO.
Y-YAKUMO-KUN!!
WHOOSH
LOVE! IT'S LOVE!! IT'S GIVEN ME A MIRACLE!! GRAAHH!!
WHAT'S THIS?! YOU MANAGED TO SURVIVE ONE OF MY PUNCHES?!
D-DOES THIS MEAN MY LOVE IS INFERIOR TO HIS?!
Same Comment.

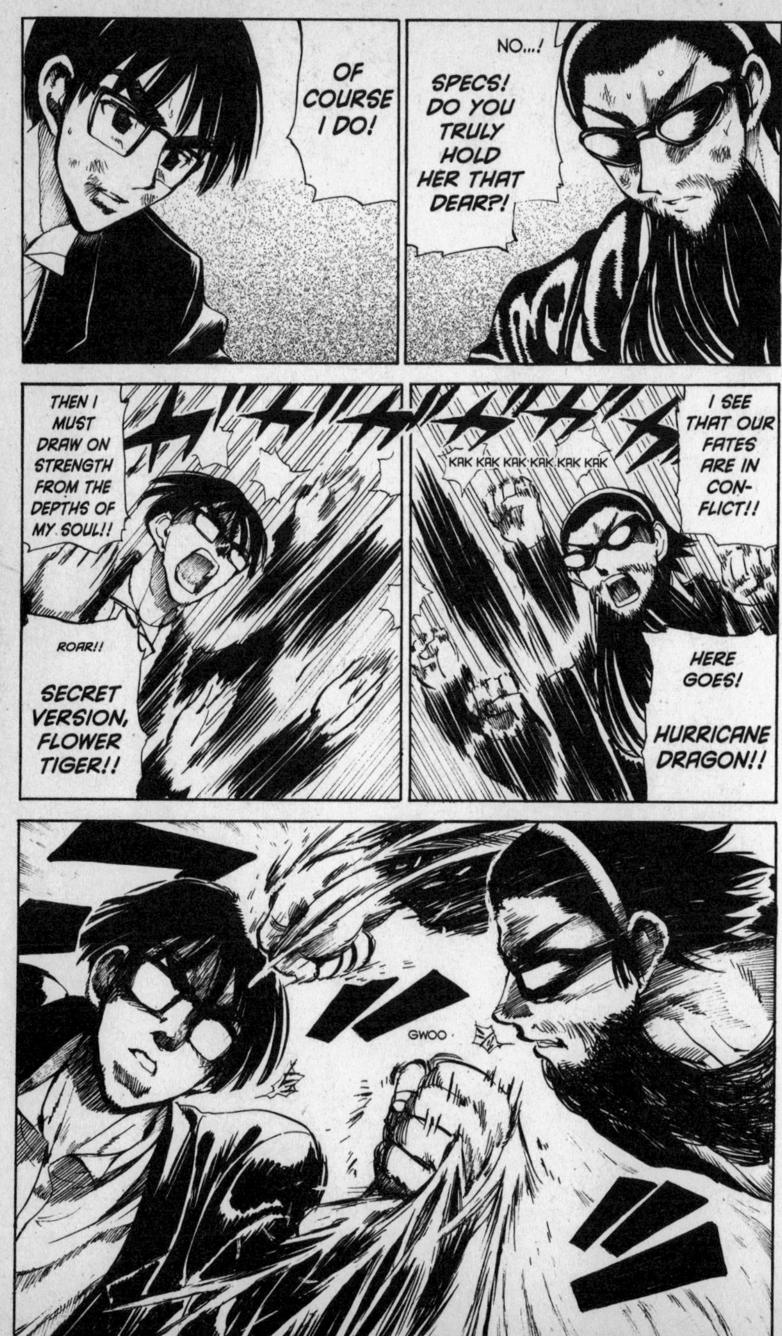

Both Have Ultimate Attacks.

And Only a Friendship Deepens.

 # 63 . . . . Fin

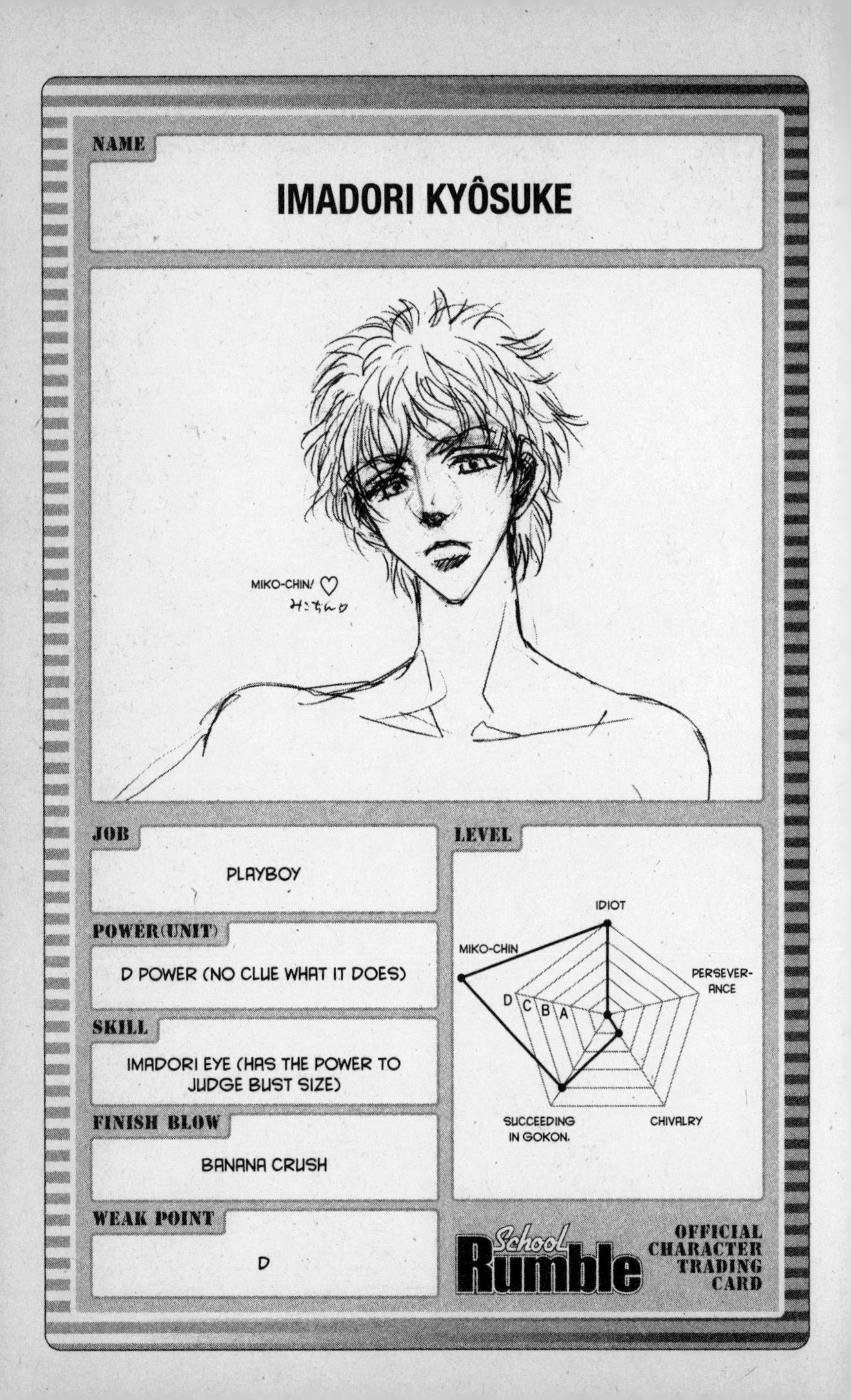
NAME
IMADORI KYÔSUKE
MIKO-CHIN! ♡
みこちん♡
JOB
PLAYBOY
POWER(UNIT)
D POWER (NO CLUE WHAT IT DOES)
SKILL
IMADORI EYE (HAS THE POWER TO JUDGE BUST SIZE)
FINISH BLOW
BANANA CRUSH
WEAK POINT
D
LEVEL
IDIOT
MIKO-CHIN
PERSEVER-ANCE
D
C
B
A
SUCCEEDING IN GOKON.
CHIVALRY
School Rumble
OFFICIAL CHARACTER TRADING CARD

64 PERSONA

Girl Fight: Round Two.

Sawachika Eri: Always Has Opinions on Other People's Love Lives.

HUMPH! HE'S SHALLOW.
YOU HAVE THE RIGHT TO SAY THAT?
PEEP PEEP PEEP
I'M NOT SHALLOW.
IT ISN'T LIKE I'M ASKING *THEM* OUT.
HM? WHAT?
DON'T YOU ALWAYS SAY THAT WE SHOULD "EXPERIENCE AS MANY LOVES AS WE CAN"?
NO, THAT'S NOT THE POINT. IT'S JUST THAT HE'S SO FLIPPANT.
THERE'S SOMETHING I SHOULD REMEMBER!
WHAT IS IT?
YOU'VE ALSO SAID, "PEOPLE ARE FREE TO LOVE HOW THEY LIKE."
AND PEOPLE HAVE ALL SORTS OF WAYS, DON'T THEY?
YES, I KNOW ALL THAT, BUT...
POPEEEN
THEN YOU WANT MIKOTO ALL TO YOURSELF?
GAME OVER!
EH?!
BUT...
DON'T THEY LOOK LIKE A HUSBAND-WIFE COMEDY TEAM?
AND MIKO-CHAN DOESN'T SEEM TO HATE HIM AS MUCH AS SHE PRETENDS TO.
MIKOTO? NO, I DON'T THINK SO.
HUH? WHY NOT?
YOU NEVER KNOW!
SOMETHING HAPPENED BETWEEN THOSE TWO WHEN WE WENT CAMPING!
IN THE TEST OF COURAGE!
OH, THAT.
SHE REALLY WASN'T INTERESTED IN TALKING ABOUT IT, HUH?
THAT GIRL.
COULD IT BE?

In Three Bags, Three Kinds of Love Were Contained. Supposedly.

YEAH...I WANTED TO MAKE YOU APPLE BUNNIES TO CHEER YOU ON YOUR DATE, BUT AFTER TRYING TO WORK WITH THE KNIFE, I STOPPED. BUT I KNEW THAT YOU'D BE OKAY BECAUSE YOU WERE KARERIN!
THANK GOODNESS!!
YEAH. THANKS TO YOU, IT WAS AN EASY VICTORY!
I CRUSHED IT, BUT...
AH! BY THE WAY, HOW'D IT GO? WAS IT A BIG SUCCESS?!
LET'S IGNORE THE MASK FOR A MOMENT.
EH? Y-YEAH, JUST A LITTLE. WE MIGHT HAVE COME A LITTLE CLOSER...
IMADORI-SAN MIGHT NOT SHARE THAT OPINION, BUT...
HEEEY! THAT'S GREAT!!
THAT'S SO GREAT! IT WENT SO WELL, I'M JEALOUS!
YEAH, YEAH.
AND FROM NOW ON, YOU AND IMADORI-KUN CAN...
AAAHH!!
TWIK
ビクッ
EH?
WHAT?
......
WHAT'S WRONG, TSUKAMOTO-SAN?
SHUFFLE SHUFFLE
わなわな...
UH...UHH...
I-I FORGOT!!
I- IMADORI-KUN IS IN LOVE WITH MIKO-CHAN...!!!

Karerin: Now Watching Dojibiron Regularly.

G-GIVE IT YOUR BEST, OKAY...?
VWIP
SURE!
THANK YOU SO MUCH, TSUKAMOTO-SAN!
SEE YOU!
VWIP
T-TAKE CARE...!
...... BYE...
TMP TMP TMP
WH-WHAT'LL I DO...?!!
AFTER SCHOOL...
2 - C
AWW! I'M RESPONSIBLE FOR ALL THIS! AND JUST A FEW MINUTES AGO, IMADORI AND MIKO-CHAN LOOKED SO CLOSE, I WAS LIGHTHEARTEDLY ROOTING THEM ON!
AND WHAT'S WITH YOU, DARNED THUMB! BAD THUMB! BAD THUMB!
KARERIN IS IN LOVE WITH IMADORI-KUN. BUT IMADORI-KUN IS IN LOVE WITH MIKO-CHAN.
THIS IS NOT GOING WELL AT ALL!
Tsukamoto Tenma: Queen of the Busybodies.

I WONDER WHAT IMADORI-KUN THINKS OF ALL THIS.
HEY, BEAUTIFUL!
WHAT ARE YOU DOING AFTER THIS?
MUSCLE
HOW ABOUT A DATE?
WHAMM
OW!!!
WHAT WAS THAT FOR?!
SHUT YOUR MOUTH!!
HUMPH
VATT
MUSCLE
LISTEN VERY CLOSELY!! THERE IS SOMEBODY WHO THINKS ONLY OF YOU...
WATCHES THE SAME PROGRAMS IMADORI WATCHES.
MMFL!
MUSCLE
GAMPH

Dojibiron's Ultimate Attack: Recruiting.

 # 64 . . . . Fin

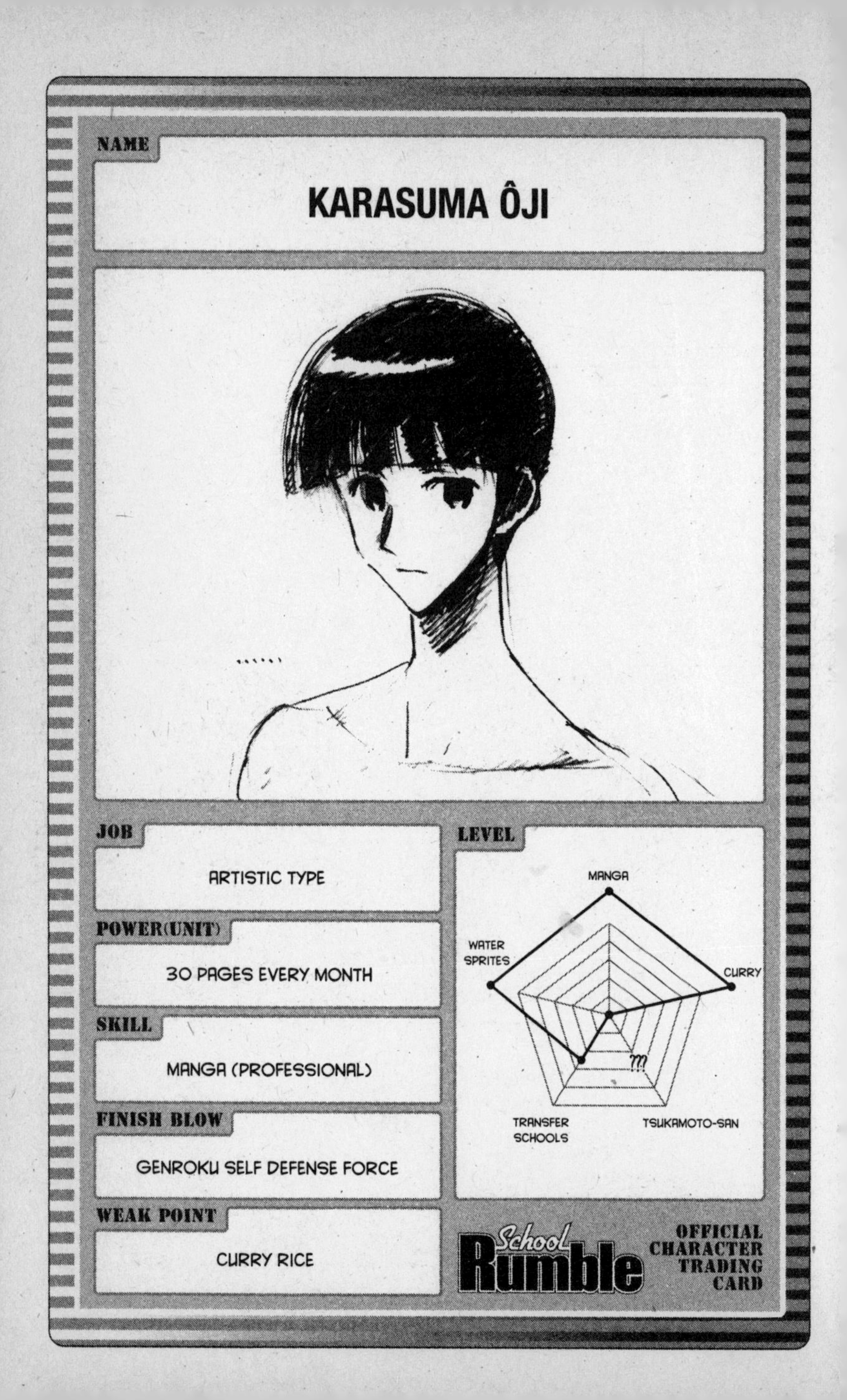
NAME
KARASUMA ÔJI
......
JOB
ARTISTIC TYPE
POWER(UNIT)
30 PAGES EVERY MONTH
SKILL
MANGA (PROFESSIONAL)
FINISH BLOW
GENROKU SELF DEFENSE FORCE
WEAK POINT
CURRY RICE
LEVEL
MANGA
CURRY
???
TSUKAMOTO-SAN
TRANSFER SCHOOLS
WATER SPRITES
School Rumble
OFFICIAL CHARACTER TRADING CARD

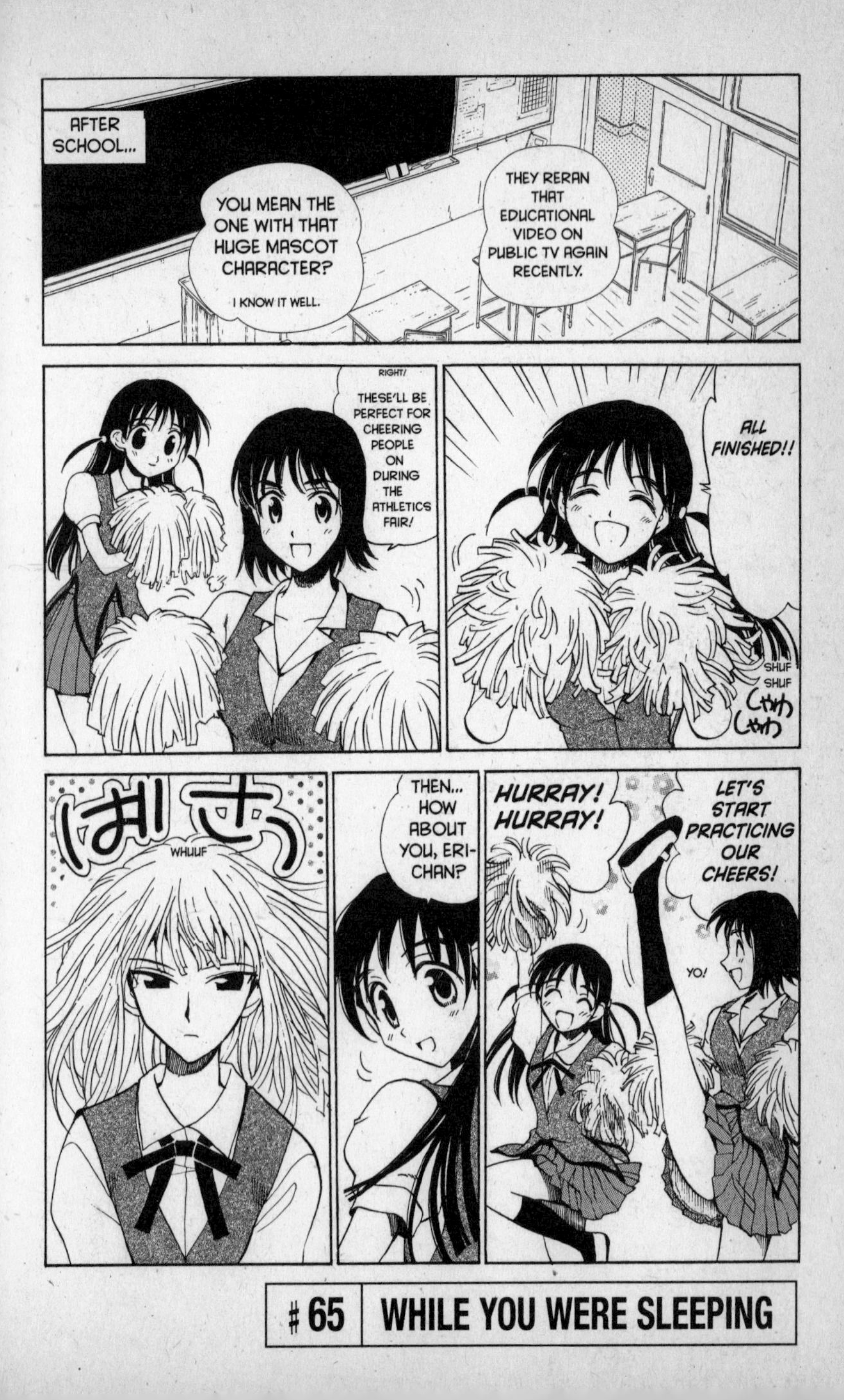

AFTER SCHOOL...
THEY RERAN THAT EDUCATIONAL VIDEO ON PUBLIC TV AGAIN RECENTLY.
YOU MEAN THE ONE WITH THAT HUGE MASCOT CHARACTER?
I KNOW IT WELL.
ALL FINISHED!!
SHUF SHUF
しゃわ しゃわ
RIGHT!
THESE'LL BE PERFECT FOR CHEERING PEOPLE ON DURING THE ATHLETICS FAIR!
LET'S START PRACTICING OUR CHEERS!
HURRAY! HURRAY!
YO!
THEN... HOW ABOUT YOU, ERI-CHAN?
WHUUF

#65 WHILE YOU WERE SLEEPING

ZWITCH
K-SNIP
K-SNIP
K-SNIP
WOOW! AMAZING! AKIRA-CHAN, YOU'RE CUTE!
SAWACHIKA! I'M IMPRESSED!
THAT'S ABOUT WHAT I WANTED.
SNIPP
EH?

She Didn't Do It on Purpose.

Sawachika Eri: Holds a Number of Grudges.
H-HEH, HEH!
THERE IT IS.
HEY! WHAT ARE WE GOING TO DO?
YOU MEAN WITH THE BEARD?
COME ON! TALK IN A WHISPER!
VLMM
..... HMM... QUIT TALKING SO LOUD, HUH...
MUMBLE MUMBLE
SAFE... !!
PHEW
HARIMA REALLY IS IN LOVE WITH THAT BEARD, ISN'T HE?
LIKE IT'S HIS GRANDCHILD!
YES. HE'S ALWAYS STROKING IT LIKE IT'S A PET. HE ALSO WENT ON ABOUT MAINTAINING IT.
MNSH MNSH
WH-WH-WHAT DID YOU DO THAT FOR?
DO YOU HAVE SOME KIND OF GRUDGE AGAINST HIM?
I-IT WAS JUST AN ACCIDENT! AN ACCIDENT!
AN ACCIDENT?!
HEY! THIS IS REALLY BAD!!

Pretty Kenji.

......
......
...!!
MMM... MMMM... .....
MUMBLE
SAFE!!
STRUGGLE
STRUGGLE
FWMM
FWMM
WH-WH-WHAT WERE YOU DOING?!
HEY, YOU DID THE DIRTY DEED FIRST!
I DON'T KNOW PERSONALLY, BUT ISN'T A MAN'S BEARD AS IMPORTANT AS A WOMAN'S HAIR?
.....
.....!
......
I GET THE FEELING THAT HIS BEARD ISN'T QUITE THAT IMPORTANT.
BUT NO MATTER.
H-HOW AM I SUPPOSED TO APOLOGIZE TO HIM?
GLANCE GLANCE
WHY DON'T YOU JUST PRETEND IGNORANCE?
THIS COULD BE FUN.
HE LOOKS SCARY, BUT HE DOESN'T GET ALL THAT ANGRY.
IF I KNOW HARIMA.
PRETENDING YOU WEREN'T INVOLVED...
MMM... MMM...
AH! HE'S WAKING UP AGAIN!!
We Predict a Coming Storm.

Taking the World by Storm, a Beard Boom.

 # 65 . . . . Fin

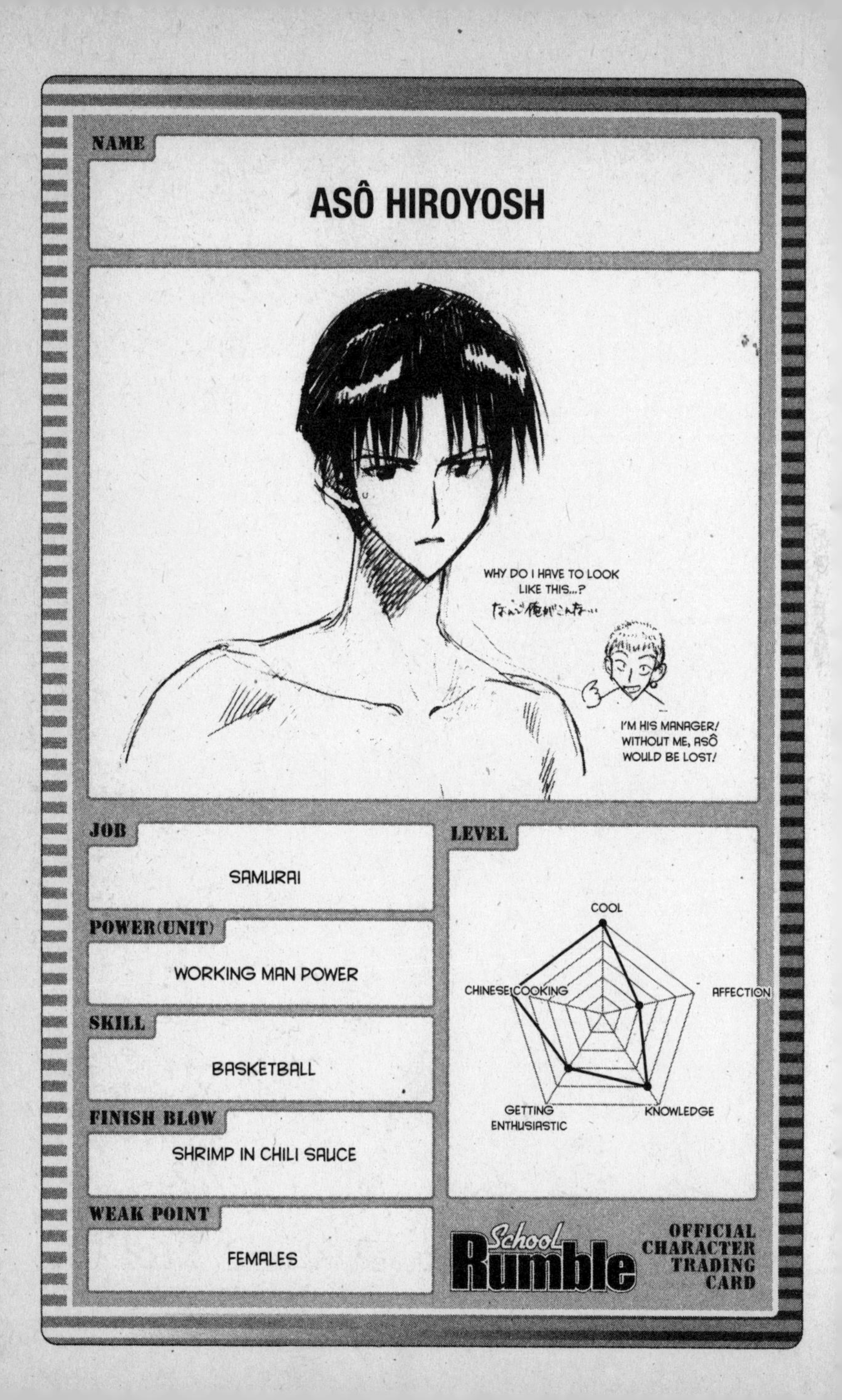
NAME
ASÔ HIROYOSH
WHY DO I HAVE TO LOOK LIKE THIS...?
なんで俺がこんな…
I'M HIS MANAGER! WITHOUT ME, ASÔ WOULD BE LOST!
JOB
SAMURAI
POWER(UNIT)
WORKING MAN POWER
SKILL
BASKETBALL
FINISH BLOW
SHRIMP IN CHILI SAUCE
WEAK POINT
FEMALES
LEVEL
COOL
AFFECTION
KNOWLEDGE
GETTING ENTHUSIASTIC
CHINESE COOKING
School Rumble
OFFICIAL CHARACTER TRADING CARD

66 THE RAZOR'S EDGE

WHAT DID YOU COME HERE FOR?
"WHAT"...? I WANTED TO APOLO--
GO AWAY.
EH?
I DON'T WANT TO SEE YOUR FACE! GO AWAY!
HEY! WHAT *IS* THIS?!
THAT'S AN AWFUL THING TO SAY!
ESPECIALLY TO A GIRL!
YOU DON'T EVEN INTEND TO HEAR ME OUT?!
THE LAST THING I WANT TO HEAR ARE YOUR CYNICAL WORDS!
I DON'T CARE! JUST GO AWAY! GET OUT OF HERE!!
SHNNK
WHOOSH
WELL, FINE!! IF THAT'S WHAT YOU WANT! HERE YOU GO ON AND ON. WHAT KIND OF MAN ARE YOU? WELL, IT'S MY OWN FAULT FOR WANTING TO APOLOGIZE!
FOR PITY'S SAKE!
EH?
THEN YOU REALLY CAME TO MAKE FUN OF ME AGAIN, HUH?
HUMPH!
HEH, HEH, HEH... IF THAT'S IT, THEN IT'S A NEW GAME.
WHFF

LISTEN, PRINCESS...
YOU'VE COMMITTED A SERIOUS MISTAKE...
...DON'T YOU KNOW THAT?
I DO KNOW IT.
I'M HOPING THAT THERE'S SOMETHING I CAN DO...
OH, HO! A WISE DECISION.
THEN YOU WILL DO AS I SAY.
DOOM
EH...?
IT IS SIMPLE.
FROM TODAY ON, YOU WILL BE MY LITTLE SISTER.
HYOOOO
OK?
HARIMA HAS A TENDENCY TO MIX ENGLISH WITH HIS JAPANESE.
HUH? WHAT DOES THAT MEAN?
YOUR MISTRESS?
MY UNDERLING!! COME ON! LEARN A LITTLE ABOUT THE PUNK LIFESTYLE!
WH-WHAT EXACTLY AM I SUPPOSED TO DO?
HM... WELL, FOR START-ERS...
HEH HEH HEH HEH
GO BUY ME SOME TEA!

Sawachika Eri: Obedient This Time.

Positions Reversed...

THIS MAY TAKE A LITTLE TIME, SO JUST HANG IN THERE A WHILE.
I'LL HAVE IT DELIVERED.
BEEP
BEEP
NO. UH...
NEVER MIND. REALLY.
DAMMIT. I UNDERESTIMATED THE RICH.
I NEVER EXPECTED HER TO REALIZE THAT I HAVE ONLY THE DREAMS OF A GUY IN POVERTY.
UHHHN
NO, WAIT. I'M RIGHT ABOUT THIS. CALM, CALM.
......!
HEY, PRINCESS.
WHAT? AND STOP CALLING ME PRINCESS.
ACTUALLY, I HAVE A HAT THAT WOULD LOOK GREAT ON YOU.
WHY DON'T YOU TRY IT ON?
EH...?
...Ends in Failure.
HM.
I DON'T MIND.
BWA HA HA HA HA HA!!
OOH HYA HYA HYA HYA
IT SUITS YOU PERFECTLY!

TENMA-CHAN...
I KNOW THAT YOU'LL BE DISAPPOINTED TO SEE ME WITHOUT MY BEARD.
AND THAT WAS ONE OF THE POINTS ABOUT ME YOU LIKED!
I'M AFRAID FOR YOU TO SEE ME NOW.
....
I'M JUST TERRIBLE AT APOLOGIES...
YES, THAT'S ME.
..... HEY, BEARD!
MM?

HOW LONG ARE YOU GOING TO SLEEP THERE?
EH?
I FIGURED...
...THAT I'D COME UP AND APOLOGIZE.
I'M SORRY.
F- FORGET ABOUT IT.
IT DOESN'T DO ME ANY GOOD TO GET MAD AT YOU.
COME ON! CAN'T YOU JUST ACCEPT AN APOLOGY?
BESIDES, WHY WERE YOU SO ATTACHED TO THAT BEARD?
......
MOST PEOPLE LOOK BETTER WITHOUT IT.
SOME-BODY IN MY FAMILY HAS ONE TOO, BUT IT ISN'T THE BEST IMAGE TO LEAVE.
HUMPH!
IT DOESN'T MATTER WHAT *YOU* THINK ABOUT IT!
I'M GOING TO GROW IT AGAIN! ONE MORE TIME!

KACHAK
ERI-CHAN!!
!!
WE CAME UP TO SEE HOW YOU DID!
WITH HARIMA-KUN.
IT LOOKS LIKE IT DIDN'T GO VERY WELL...
SHHT
OH, FOR...
YOU GUYS CAME JUST IN TIME.
THERE'S SOMETHING I WANT TO ASK.
?
BETWEEN THOSE GUYS WITH BEARDS AND THOSE WITHOUT...
...WHICH DO YOU LIKE BEST?
WITHOUT!
ABSOLUTELY CERTAIN.
AS I WAS SAYING...
ARE YOU LISTENING TO ME?!
HEY!
GRMMP

Forgiveness: Not in the Cards.

 # 66 .... Fin

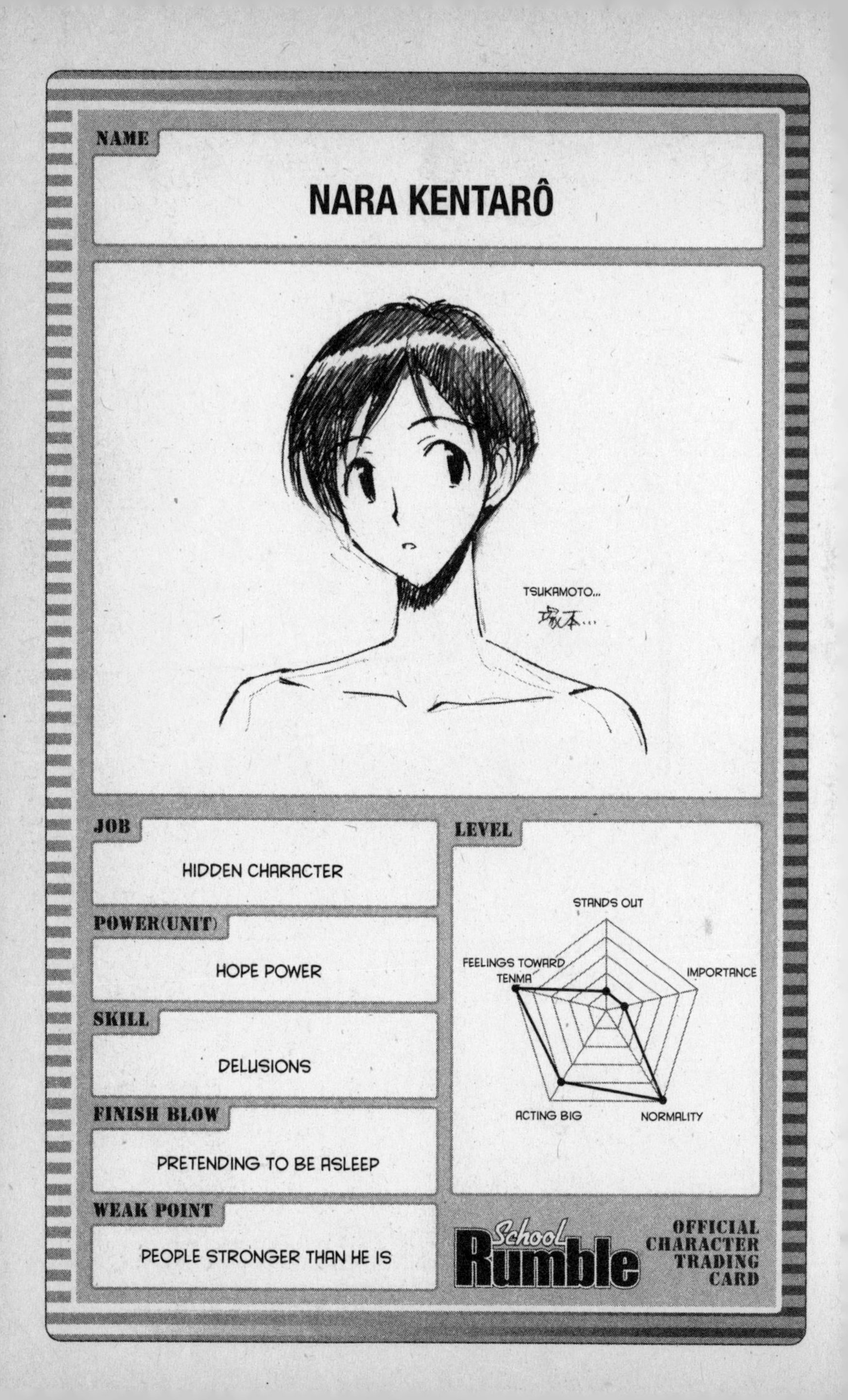
NAME
NARA KENTARÔ
TSUKAMOTO...
塚本…
JOB
HIDDEN CHARACTER
POWER(UNIT)
HOPE POWER
SKILL
DELUSIONS
FINISH BLOW
PRETENDING TO BE ASLEEP
WEAK POINT
PEOPLE STRONGER THAN HE IS
LEVEL
STANDS OUT
IMPORTANCE
NORMALITY
ACTING BIG
FEELINGS TOWARD TENMA
School Rumble
OFFICIAL CHARACTER TRADING CARD

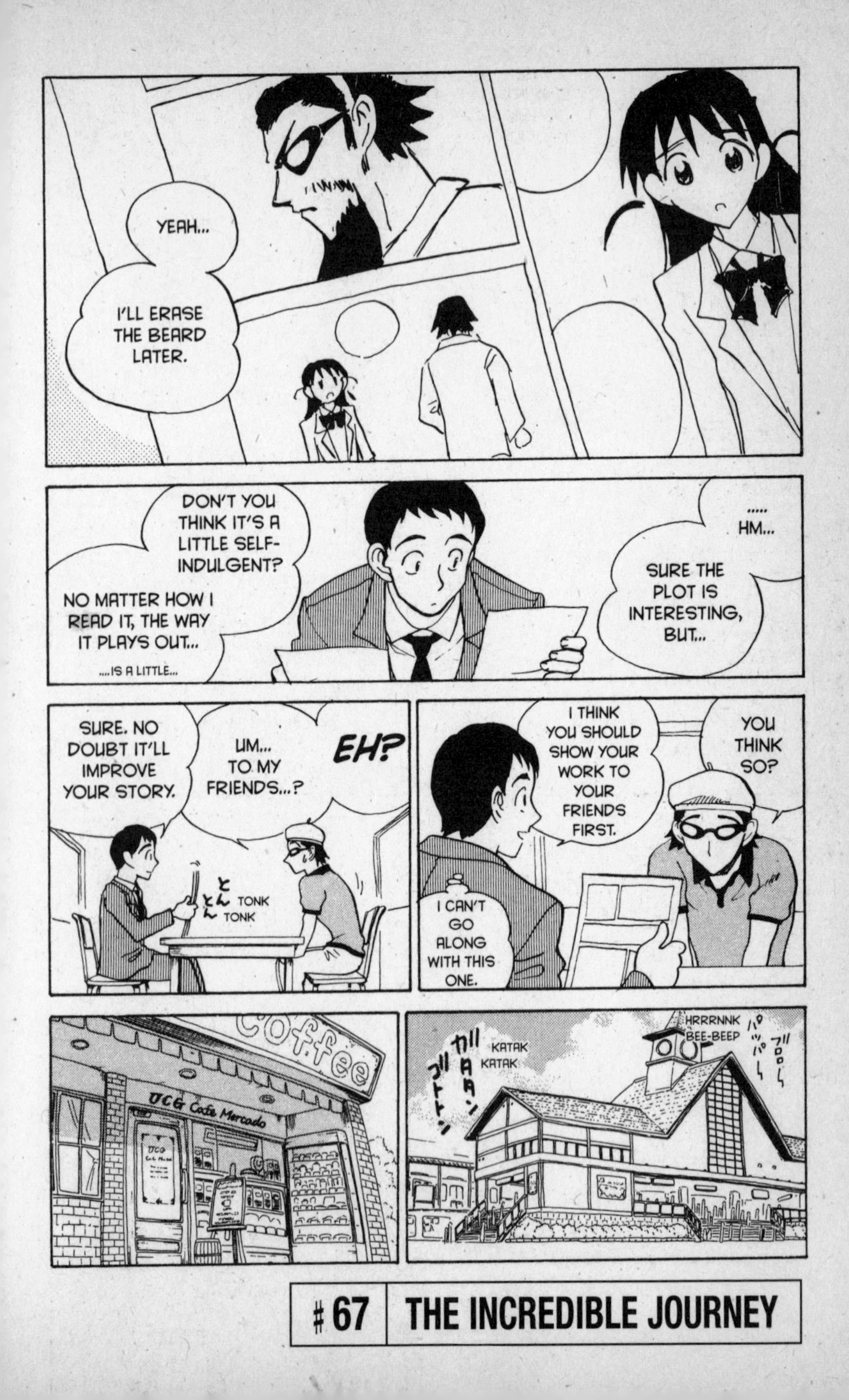

#67 THE INCREDIBLE JOURNEY

DAMMIT! I GUESS THERE'RE LIMITS TO LEARNING ON YOUR OWN.
FRIENDS... I'VE MADE IT THIS FAR, BUT I'VE GOT A HUGE WALL BEFORE ME!
WHY AM I DRAWING MANGA ANYWAY?
THERE IS NOBODY LIKE THAT, YOU IDIOT!!
I'M A DELINQUENT!
BAMM
ITOKO...? NO, I COULDN'T. I'D BE TOO EMBAR-RASSED!
IT'S LIKE SHOWING YOUR DIARY TO YOUR FAMILY!
PYOTR AND THE GANG...? THEY'D NEVER BE INTERESTED IN A BEAUTIFUL LOVE STORY SUCH AS THIS!
COULD THEY EVEN UNDERSTAND?
WHO ELSE...
けけけ HA HA HA
けけけけ HA HA HA HA
BUWOOM BUWOOM
ぼわん ぼわん
I COULD NEVER SHOW THEM!!
BAMM
びくっ!! AK!
GA HA HA HA!!
くけけけ!!
THE PRINCESS SHAVED MY HEAD!
SKRAAAPE
I'M AT A STAGE IN MY LIFE WITH A LOT OF WORRIES.
TSK!
HM?
ISN'T THAT...?!

WHA-?!
THAT'S "MANGO-KU"?!
WHY WOULD A BIG STAR BE IN A PLACE LIKE THIS?
ZOOM
ダッ
IMPOS-SIBLE!!
BUT IT'S DEFINITELY HIM!
YAKUSHA-MARU!!
DING DING
カラン カラン
MANGO-KU! WAIT UP!!
DID HE FORGET THIS?
DING DING
カラン カラン
I-I MET THE GUY IN THE FLESH!
HAHH
ハア!!
HAHH
ハア!!
I FIGURED HE'D BE BUSY, SO I ONLY EXPECTED HIM TO SAY HI.
BUT HE WAS NICE ENOUGH TO GIVE ME AN AUTO-GRAPH!
DAMN! I DON'T KNOW WHERE I GOT THE LUCK!
Yakushamaru Kôji: Star of "Three to Get Killed!"
3

LET'S SEE... HIS NAME IS...
SST
GRATCH
TWIK
HAHH
HAHH
HAHH
....
U-UM...
......
DID YOU SEE?!
GLARE

H-HARIMA-SAN...
H- HELLO...
YOU'RE YOUNGER-SISTER-SAN! I NEVER THOUGHT YOU'D BE WORKING HERE! HOW UNEXPECTED!
AND HOW ADMIRABLE.
COULD YOU LOCK THIS INCIDENT INSIDE YOU AND NEVER LET IT OUT?!
Y-YEAH...
GRIMP
I-I WILL.
STCH
THEN I'LL SAY GOODBYE.
......
TWIRL
TMP
TMP
TMP
GRIMP
TWTCH
STARRE
...... U...
UM...?
A LITTLE AFRAID.
WELL?
WHAT DID YOU THINK?
HUH?
I MEAN... OF THE MANGA?

ズズ
SL-SLUUUURP
……
ドキドキ
B-BMP B-BMP
……
!
AH! IT'S THAT PAGE!
OKAY, NOW LAUGH!
……
……
B-BMP B-BMP B-BMP B-BMP B-BMP B-BMP
WHA?!
パラ
FLIP
SH-SHE JUST READ IT STRAIGHT THROUGH?!
……
IMPOSSIBLE!
WHAT IS GOING ON?!
……
!
じろ
GLARRRE
……
……
…… U-UM…
AH! N-NO! NOTHING!
IT WAS NOTHING AT ALL!
I'LL JUST LOOK OVER HERE.
YEAH!
A LITTLE SCARED.
TWIRL

It Is Self-Indulgent.
FLIP パラ…
……
GLANCE ちら
ちら
TH-THE NEXT PAGE IS THE BIGGEST HIGHLIGHT OF THE PIECE!
GLANCE そわそわ FIDGET FIDGET
どきどきどき B-BMP B-BMP B-BMP
FLIP パラ…
!
AH!
RIGHT! WE HAVE A REACTION!!
ゴク! GULP
THE PAGES ARE MIXED UP.
PAGE 6 IS PAGE 9, AND...
THIS CAN'T BE HAPPENING!!!
EYAAAH!
ばんばん BAM BAM
HAHHH HAHHH
……
SCARY...
カランッ KACHINK
……
WELL?
どきどき… B-BMP B-BMP
ゴク… GULP
WHAT DO YOU THINK?
ビクッ TWIK
..... U-UM...
IT WAS GOOD...
SHE'S LYING!!
I CAN TELL! BUT I'M NOT GOING TO LET HER PUT ONE OVER ON ME!!
....
B-BUT... THE MAIN CHARACTER GUY IS A LITTLE...
...SELFISH AND VIOLENT... MAYBE...?
THERE!
NOW THE TRUTH COMES OUT!!
ZING
QUICKLY GETS SCARED
GM GM GM GM GM

IT'S TERRIBLE!
I KNEW IT! I'M USELESS AT THIS KIND OF WORK!
I'M NOTHING MORE THAN A DELINQUENT AFTER ALL! I SHOULD NEVER FORGET MY PLACE IN LIFE!
HA...OKAY, FINE! I'LL WASH MY HANDS OF THIS, AND FROM TOMORROW ON, I'LL GET SERIOUS ABOUT WHAT I...
STILL...
I DON'T KNOW WHAT OTHER PEOPLE WOULD THINK OF IT, BUT...
I...KIND OF LIKE GUYS LIKE THAT.
......
EH?
ANOTHER THING...
THAT GUY'S SECRET...
DON'T YOU THINK HE NEEDS A FRIEND HE CAN CONFIDE IN?
GASHANN!!
!
U-UM, I'M SORRY!
AN AMATEUR HAS NO RIGHT TO PRETEND TO UNDER-STAND...
THUMP
TWICH

THAT'S IT!!
KLNCH
EH?
I CAN'T JUST SIT HERE ANYMORE!!
SORRY, BUT I HAVE TO GO HOME!
I HAVE TO REDRAW THE STORY!
KATAK KATAK
R-- RIGHT...
THANKS FOR THE HELP, SISTER-SAN.
WHEN I'M FINISHED, I'LL COME BY AGAIN.
EH?
IF YOU DON'T MIND, I'D LIKE YOU TO READ IT AGAIN.
......!!
O-OKAY!
I WISH I HAD SOMETHING TO GIVE YOU IN THANKS.
BUT THIS IS THE ONLY THING I HAVE.
......
EH? YOU REALLY WANT IT?
AN AUTOGRAPH FROM MANGOKU!!!
WHO'D YOU GET THIS FROM?!
....
IT'S A SECRET...
Mangoku: He's So Popular!
67 .... Fin

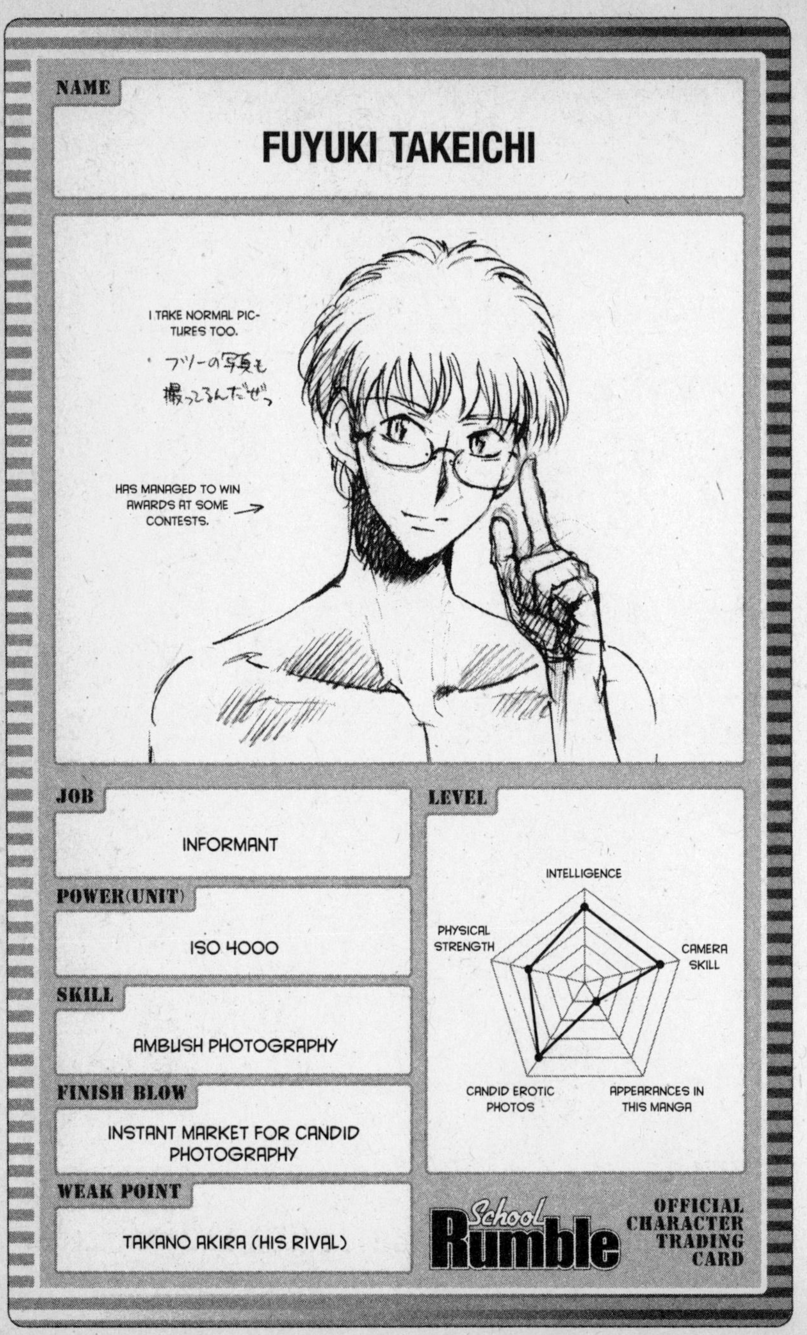
NAME
FUYUKI TAKEICHI
I TAKE NORMAL PICTURES TOO.
フツーの写真も撮ってるんだぜっ
HAS MANAGED TO WIN AWARDS AT SOME CONTESTS.
JOB
INFORMANT
POWER(UNIT)
ISO 4000
SKILL
AMBUSH PHOTOGRAPHY
FINISH BLOW
INSTANT MARKET FOR CANDID PHOTOGRAPHY
WEAK POINT
TAKANO AKIRA (HIS RIVAL)
LEVEL
INTELLIGENCE
CAMERA SKILL
APPEARANCES IN THIS MANGA
CANDID EROTIC PHOTOS
PHYSICAL STRENGTH
School Rumble
OFFICIAL CHARACTER TRADING CARD

AFTER SCHOOL...
THE PEOPLE PARTICIPATING IN THE SCHOOL ATHLETICS FAIR RACES ARE PRETTY MUCH DECIDED.
WE HAVE OUR BATTLE LINES SET!
WONDERFUL, IF I SAY SO MYSELF.
NEXT IS THE CLASS-VS.-CLASS RELAY. A PRETTY IMPORTANT RACE.
WE NEED FIVE NAMES, MALE OR FEMALE.
WE'LL FIND OUR RUNNERS QUICKLY.
ALL RIGHT! WHO HERE IS FAST?
WHO'S GOOD AT THE 100 METER?
WELL, UME IS A SHOO-IN.
OTHER THAN THAT, THERE'S HANAI, ASÔ...SUGA, MAYBE?
ざわ ざわ
CHATTER CHATTER
FOR THE GIRLS MADOKA... SUÔ-SAN, SAWACHIKA-SAN...
WHO ELSE...?
You Knew It.
AKIRA!
WHY DON'T YOU COMPETE!
I HAVE ONE CONDITION...
I'D LIKE...
I CHANGED MY MIND.
HEY, WHAT ABOUT IMADORI?
I THOUGHT HE WAS PRETTY FAST...
カタ カタ カタ...
CHIK CHIK CHIK
68 MOUSE HUNT

Imadori: Hoping for the Baton Touch of Love.

BY THE WAY...
WHERE'S THE BIG GUY... HARIMA?
AAAH! DON'T ASK QUESTIONS WE DON'T WANT TO ANSWER!
ACTUALLY, EVERYBODY THOUGHT HE MIGHT BE GOOD.
BUT HE'D NEVER ENTER IN A RACE. NO WAY!
YEAH...HE LOOKS LIKE HE'D BE FAST.
BUT HE ISN'T HERE.
I WONDER WHERE HE WENT?
IMADORI, GET HARIMA ON THE PHONE.
DON'T GO AROUND GIVING ME ORDERS. YOU'RE MAKING ME MAD!
HE COULD JUST MAKE THE CALL HIMSELF!
BESIDES, I...
...HAVE NO IDEA WHAT HIS NUMBER IS.
YOU DON'T EITHER?
ざわっ…!
CHATTER
I THOUGHT THEY WERE FRIENDS...

Takano Akira: Why…
MAYBE HE'S BEATEN THE ODDS AND DOESN'T HAVE ONE.
A CELL PHONE.
NOPE, HE HAS ONE.
..... HOW DO YOU KNOW?
YOU CAN'T BE...
BECAUSE I KNOW HIS NUMBER.
OH! DO YOU WANT IT?
NO, I DON'T!
WHAT I MEAN IS, YOU SHOULD GIVE THE NUMBER TO HANAI AND THOSE GUYS.
HMM... WELL, I'D LIKE TO...
BUT I JUST DON'T FEEL LIKE HELPING OUT HANAI.
WHEN I SEE THAT SCHOOL SPIRIT, I JUST CAN'T...
IF YOU KNOW THE NUMBER, THEN HELP THEM OUT!
THEY'RE TRYING THEIR HARD-EST, RIGHT?
SIGH
THAT HARIMA! NOT EVEN A GLIMMER OF COOPERA-TION!
IF THAT'S HOW HE WANTS IT, I'LL FIND HIM AND FORCE HIM INTO THE RACE!
I'D JUST LEAVE HIM ALONE.
SHKK
NO PATIENCE FOR THOSE WHO AREN'T WITH THE PLAN.
SORRY, BUT TAKE OVER FOR ME.
SHUMMP
EH? WAIT!
HUMPH!
STMP
STMP
HE'S PROBABLY SLEEPING ON THE ROOF AS ALWAYS!

THE ROOF...
I MEAN...
SORRY ABOUT THIS...
CALLING YOU UP HERE LIKE THIS.
IT'S OKAY.
MY CLASSES WERE OVER ANYWAY.
BUT YOU WERE SURPRISED, RIGHT?
THAT I SUDDENLY SENT YOU A TEXT MESSAGE.
AND UP TO THE ROOF.
AH...
YES... I HAVE TO SAY I WAS...
ESPECIALLY WHEN THE SUBJECT SAID, "TOSSING THE SCREEN TONE AWAY."
WELL, WHAT DO YOU THINK?
I WOULD VERY MUCH LIKE TO HEAR YOUR CANDID OPINION.
AH!
YES...
THE PROBLEM IS THIS SCENE HERE.
IN THE CLIMAX, THE HERO YELLS OUT TO THE HEROINE TO STOP HER, RIGHT?
SEE? HERE.
YES...

KACHAK
HM!
I KNEW THAT JERK HARIMA WOULD BE HERE!
HM?
HE'S WITH SOME-ONE, AND SHE'S...
HOW ABOUT A KISS RIGHT HERE. WOULD YOU LIKE THAT?
UM...
UH...
YES.
I THINK THAT WOULD BE PERFECT.

SNAPP
EVERY-BODY SHUT UP!!!
BAM
STPP
MAI-CHAN! MAI-CHAN!
CONTROL YOURSELF!
.....?
HM? WHAT'S THE MATTER?
NOTH-ING...
I JUST HAD THE FEELING THAT SOMEONE WAS THERE.
OH! SORRY. MAYBE WHOEVER IT WAS GOT THE WRONG IDEA.
A MAN AND WOMAN IN THIS SITUATION.
AH! NO, I DON'T MIND...
BUT... THERE WAS SOME-THING...IT'S HARD TO DESCRIBE...
THERE WAS THIS HUGE THOUGHT...
HUH? THOUGHT?
N-NO... IT'S NOTHING...
Mai-chan: Class Representative.

HANAI NEVER RETURNED TO THE CLASS-ROOM.
IN THE END, HANAI NEVER CAME BACK.
COULD HE AND HARIMA HAVE HAD SOME PROB-LEM?
BUT I'VE GOT NO REASON TO CALL HIM.
SHUMMP
WHA- !!
WHAT IS THIS?!
ZAAA
TIKKA TIKKA
GM
GM
GM
GM
GM

The Hanai Family Prepares for War.

 # 68· · · · · · · · ·Fin

School
Rumble

69
THE MCKENZIE BREAK
GRAW! GRAW!
ギャアッ ギャアッ
ドドドドド…
SHHHHHH
HYUUUU
クォー
SHHHHH
ドドドドド
HE WAS SUPPOSED TO BE AROUND HERE.
HM?
WHAT IS THAT?!
ドン
DOOM
GRRN GRRN
ギチギチ
KH!
GLIPP
チャプ…

GWOOM
HAA!!
チャプン
GLUPP
SLRRP
チョロ
3559 TIMES!!
GWUMMM
HEY! I TOLD YOU THAT YOUR MOVES HAVE TO BE GRACE-FUL!!
THAT HAS TO BE THE TOUGHEST TRAINING I'VE EVER SEEN... BUT...
YOU MUST BRING THE WATER TO THE UPPER BOWLS WITHOUT SPILLING A DROP!!
UNNN!!

Suô Mikoto: Worried About Her Childhood Friend.
S-SOMETHING'S CHANGED.
THIS ISN'T THE USUAL CALM HANAI. YES...HE'S ALMOST LIKE A WILD BEAST!
WH-WHAT COULD HAVE HAPPENED TO YOU?!
HANAI!!
KH!!
HAVE YOU NOTICED?
HE IS VERY MUCH AKIN TO A NAKED SWORD.
YES... HE HAS LOST ALL REASON AND IS NOW A BEAST, HUNGRY FOR BLOOD...
SHHHHH
DEEP IN HIS HEART...
...HE IS BATTLING HIS OWN EVIL!!
WHA--?!
HEH, HEH, HEH... WHEN ONE HAS LOST ONE'S "SELF," ONE CAN NO LONGER TRAVEL DOWN THE PATH...
HOWEVER, LOVE MAKES A MAN MUCH STRONGER.
HEH, HEH...BUT THIS WON'T GO THE WAY HE THINKS IT WILL.

STILL, LET'S DISPENSE WITH THE DIFFICULT CON-CEPTS.
YOUNG LADY, IF YOU WANT TO DEFEAT HIM, NOW IS THE TIME.
EH?!
I-I'M NOT HERE TO DO ANY-THING LIKE THAT!
HEH, HEH... YOU ARE STRONG, BUT BECAUSE OF THAT, YOU DON'T SHOW THE MEN HOW WOMANLY YOU ARE.
BUT HE'S THE TYPE OF MAN WHO KNOWS THAT.
HAHHH
UM-HM. THAT'S ENOUGH FOR TODAY.
HEH, HEH... STAY IF YOU LIKE, I MUST LEAVE.
HAHH
HAHH
HEY!
S-SUÔ...! WHAT ARE YOU DOING HERE...?
YOU HAVEN'T BEEN BACK FOR TWO DAYS!
TWO DAYS...
HAS IT ONLY BEEN TWO DAYS...?
I COULD HAVE SWORN I'VE BEEN HERE FOR HALF A YEAR...
HAHH
HAHH
BY THE WAY... WHO WAS THAT OLD MAN?
HM?
OH, HIM...
DON'T KNOW HIM.
HUH?!

IT SEEMS HE'S SOME OLD MAN WHO LIVES WITH A FARMING FAMILY NEARBY.
HE'S GOT THIS WEIRD AURA AROUND HIM, SO I HAVEN'T TALKED TO HIM.
DON'T EVEN KNOW HIS NAME.
...... !! ...... ?!.
GRANDPA! YOU KNOW YOU CAN'T GO OUT ALONE!
YOUNG LADY, IF YOU WANT TO DEFEAT HIM, NOW IS THE TIME.
HONESTLY! YOU'RE ALWAYS WANDER-ING OFF!!
WHAMM
OW!! WHAT'D YOU HIT ME FOR?
SHUT UP! YOUR PARENTS ARE WORRIED SICK, YOU IDIOT!!
IN TOWN...
OW! OW!
GEEZ, SUÔ! WHAT'D YOU COME OUT THERE FOR ANYWAY?
I DON'T HAVE MUCH MONEY LEFT. THIS IS GOING TO MAKE IT HARD TO GET FOOD SUPPLIES...
HMM...
う~む
ONLY ONE SÔSEKI-SAN.
DAMMIT! WE YOUNG WHIPPER-SNAPPERS CAN'T LIVE OFF THE LAND ANYMORE, CAN WE?!
THE WORLD HAS NOT CHANGED AT ALL.
HA! OF COURSE IT HASN'T! WHY WOULD THE LOSS OF ONE MAN CHANGE IT?
IT'S ONLY BEEN A LITTLE OVER A DAY.
HE'S SO COOL!!
NO DOUBT ABOUT IT! HE'S NO. 1 IN MY SCHOOL!
HMM?
Suô: Still the Stronger of the Two.

Hanai's Reaction: A Bit Excessive
NOT ONLY IS HE GORGEOUS, HE'S ALSO AN ATHLETIC WIZARD!
I HEARD HE'S SO POPULAR, THEY'RE STARTING A FAN CLUB FOR HIM.
THOSE GIRLS ARE FROM MY SCHOOL... NOW THAT I THINK OF IT, I WONDER WHAT HAPPENED WITH THE ATHLETICS FAIR.
I WONDER IF *HE* JOINED IN.
THOSE SUN-GLASSES MAKE HIM LOOK DANGEROUS, BUT I LIKE THEM!
HIS LONG HAIR LOOKS SO RE-FINED! A MAN WITH DIGNITY!
I WONDER IF HE HAS A GIRLFRIEND.
MAYBE I CAN APPLY FOR THE POSITION!
I'D LOVE TO GO OUT WITH HIM...
OH, THAT HA·RI·MA·KEN·JI·SAN!
KRAKLE
WHOOM
YOU TWO!!
GRABB
Y-YES?
WHAT WERE YOU JUST SAYING? I NEED DETAILS!!
DRIPPA
DRIPPA
KYAAAAA!!!

WE WERE IN AN ALLEY BEHIND A COFFEE SHOP.
WE WERE SURROUNDED BY DELIN-QUENTS.
AND THAT'S WHEN HE ARRIVED AND SAVED US!
I THINK HE'S STILL THERE.
......
.....!!
THANK YOU!
TMP
SO THAT'S IT! I GET IT!
THAT'S HOW HE DECEIVED YAKUMO-KUN, TOO! I'M SURE OF IT!!
BUT!! I KNOW IT WAS ALL AN ACT!!
HERE YOU GO. GOOD WORK, GUYS.
HEH HEH HEH
YOU WON'T GET AWAY WITH IT!!
HAW HAW HAW
HARIMA KENJI!!!
WHOOSH
HERE IT IS!
URK!!
And His Imagination Is Excessive, Too.

DM
DM
DM
DM
I'LL REMEMBER... YOUR...NAME... HA...RI... MA...KEN...
..... YOU PRONOUNCING IT WRONG.
WHAT?!
SST
WAIT!!
VSSH
HARIMA KENJI!!

FWOOSSH
MY NAME IS...
HARRY MCKENZIE!
GLEEM
キラリーン
No Mice on the Attack This Time.
TSST
だれ
WHO?!
ツー
#69 . . . . Fin

NAME

TENNÔJI NOBORU

BEFORE YOU CAN CALL YOURSELF A PRO, THERE IS ONE MAN YOU MUST DEFEAT!!

プロになる前に…
たおさねばならん
男が居る!

JOB

MONSTER

POWER(UNIT)

MATCHLESS FIGHTER POWER

SKILL

GROWING TO GIANT SIZE

FINISH BLOW

TENNÔJI CHOP

WEAK POINT

ONLY ONE VOTE IN THE MOST POPULAR CHARACTER POLL

LEVEL

PHYSICAL STRENGTH

WISDOM

POPULARITY WITH READERS

SIZE

HAIR

School Rumble

OFFICIAL CHARACTER TRADING CARD

Harima Kenji: Bright and Sunny in His Heart.
JUST WHO ARE YOU?
HARRY MCKENZIE.
YOU CALL ME BY NAME.
BUT LISTEN, YOUNG MAN...
GLITTER
GLITTER
BEFORE ASK A PERSON'S NAME, YOU SHOULD STATE YOUR OWN.
DON'T YOU PEOPLE HAVE MANNERS IN THIS COUNTRY?
GLEEM
URK! I- I'M HANAI HARUKI...
TH- THIS DRIFTER-LIKE PERSONALITY. IS HE OLDER THAN ME?
SHKK
I HAVE ONE QUESTION... IS ALL THIS YOUR DOING?
YES. PERSONALLY, I LIKE TO LIVE LIFE IN PEACE, BUT...
UR... HE'S PUTTING ON HIS GENUINE-FOREIGNER PRESSURE!
JAPANESE PEOPLE SEEM TO LIKE FIGHTING.
IT WAS CLOSE. I WAS ALMOST INJURED.

#70 THREE VIOLENT PEOPLE

Y-YOU WON'T BEAT ME!
?
B-BUT THIS IS A LITTLE ODD.
THESE GUYS ALL HAVE DISLOCATED JOINTS...
...AND SOME HAVE BAD WOUNDS TO THEIR MID-SECTIONS.
THOSE ARE ODD INJURIES FOR DELINQUENTS.
OH, HO!
THEN YOU COUNT YOURSELF AS ONE OF THEM?
YOU ACCUSE ME OF INVITING VIOLENCE WITH THIS CROWD?
N-NO, I DIDN'T SAY THAT...
BUT THAT WHAT YOU SAYING, RIGHT?
THAT CANNOT BE POSSIBLE!
I NO THAT GOOD. HA HA HA!!
HA... HA HA HA...
WHAT THE HECK IS THIS FOREIGNER SAYING?

WHOA!!!
GWOOO
KAK
!!
HA HA! THAT A GOOD REACTION!
I SEE YOUR DOGI ISN'T JUST A COSTUME.
BUT WHAT IS IT? IT DOES NOT SEEM LIKE KARATE.
WH-WHAT?!
SO YOU THEIR BOSS.
OF COURSE YOU BE BETTER THAN THE SMALL FRY.
THAT'S HOW IT IS, HM?
EH?
BOSS?
HEY, I THINK YOU'VE GOT IT ALL WRONG!
JKK
!
TAKE A BREAK.
SST

THERE A LADY PRESENT.
?
AH...
HANAI-SEMPAI...?
YA!! Y-YAYA... YAKUMO-KUN?!
TH-THERE'S A GOOD EXPLANATION FOR ALL OF THIS! I'VE NEVER BEEN ONE TO PICK A FIGHT...
J-JUST WHAT ARE YOU HERE FOR...?
EH...? AH...
UM... ACTUALLY, I'M WORKING...
YOUNG LADY, YOU HELP ME SOME? I NEED FIND RED PLATE...
WHA--? Y-Y-Y... YOU BASTARD!!
?
TWITCH
FINE WITH ME!!
I'M YOUR ENEMY, YOU SHAMELESS CREEP!!
YOU PUT YOUR HAND ON YAKUMON'S SHOULDER, AND THAT'S AN UNFORGIVABLE CRIME!!
Yakumo's Job: Requires Many Different Costumes.

DID YOU WAIT LONG?
SORRY.
AH...
HUH?!
H-H-HARIMA AND YAKUMO-KUN IN...
...A SECRET TRYST!?
EH?!
?
AH! NO! THIS IS... YOU'RE WRONG!!
SLZT
THEN WHAT ARE YOU HERE FOR?!!
IN THIS DESERTED BACK ALLEY!!
JUST ANSWER ME THAT!!
GWOOGH
U-UM... ACTUALLY...
W-WAIT A SECOND, KENJI!!
IF THIS TALK GOES ON, MY SECRET WILL COME OUT!! AND TO THE ONE MAN I LEAST WANT TO KNOW IT!!
TREMBLE
KH!!
TREMBLE
!
SSSST
Harima Kenji: Making Good Progress on His Manga.

OF COURSE...
I'M HERE TO TAKE YOU DOWN!!
VWATT
......
YOU'RE PRE-PARED, I SEE.
NOW I'LL SHOW YOU THE FRUITS OF MY TRAINING.
SHKK
HEY, HEY!
YOU HAVE NOT THING TO DO WITH THIS! LEAVE NOW!
WHOA!!
BUMP
SHASHT
AH...!
THE PAGES...!
WAIT A BIT, SISTER-SAN.
EH...?
SHK

WHOOSH
YOU SHOULD BE THE ONE TO PICK IT UP, YOU BASTARD!!
HYAA!
HARIMA-SAN...
!
THAT GOOD PUNCH YOU HAVE.
SWMM
BUT IT USELESS IF YOU NOT HIT.
HE'S MORE THAN THE AVERAGE THUG.
!!
THWAM
キュル
GWOOM
TMP
RAH!!
HUH? H-HE'S...
?!

HYUU
KAK
ZHAAN ZHAAN
I'M THE ONE YOU'RE FIGHTING, RIGHT?
..... INTERESTING.
I THOUGHT SAMURAI WERE IN THIS COUNTRY NO MORE.

THERE'S ONE.
HAHH...
SST
IT SEEMS YOU FINALLY REALIZED.
....!!
...... WHAT'S WRONG? WHY DO YOU SHRINK BACK?
IF YOU'VE JUST NOW NOTICED HOW FEARSOME I AM, IT'S TOO LATE!
IS THIS SAMURAI...?
THAT IS A SAMURAI SAKAYAKI?
HEH... YOU SEE HOW COOL I AM?
U-UM... YOUR HAT...
PANIC
PANIC
B-BALD? IS IT HIS BALDNESS... YAKUMO-KUN?!
IS THAT WHAT STOLE YOUR HEART?
Sawachika...Holds Grudges...

♯70.........Fin

71 RENEGADE
わいわい
CHATTER
CHATTER
HEY! SHE'S HERE AGAIN! THAT WOMAN!
SHE'S HUGE!
OH... SHE'S GON-SOMETHING-OR-OTHER OF CLASS 2-D.
I HEAR SHE'S AN EXCHANGE STUDENT FROM MEXICO.
THEY SAY SHE'S OVER 170 CM! (5' 7")
I HEARD SHE'S IN THE SAME CLUB AS ICHIJÔ.
HUH? WHAT CLUB IS ICHIJÔ IN?
LUNCH... YOU EAT WITH ME.
ICHI JÔ.
EH...?

Her Name Is Lala. If You Read♭15, You'll Figure Out Who She Is.

REALLY? YOU PRACTICE TOGETHER IN THE AMATEUR WRESTLING CLUB?
LALA-CHAN WOULD BE GOOD AT IT, HUH?
WE WENT MAN-ON-MAN IN BATTLE ONCE BY MISTAKE.
MUNCH
MUNCH
ICHIJÔ, SCHOOL GIRLS DON'T TALK LIKE THAT.
HOI
SOOO... YOUR NAME IS LALA-CHAN, HUH?
AH! ICHIJÔ. I WANT THAT. THANKS.
SHE'S A FINE COMMOD-ITY!
EVEN THOUGH SHE'S AN IMPORT.
..... ICHI JÔ!
YES?
WHAT IS THIS MAN?
I FEEL A STRANGE PRESSURE FOR A WHILE NOW.
HE'S IMADORI-SAN.
HE'S A GOOD GUY.
NICE TO MEET YOU! ♫
YOU GO AWAY.
THERE'S NO NEED TO BE CRUEL...
THAT'S RIGHT!
.....
.....
HER SIZE... IT'S GOTTA BE...!!
IT'S D!!
CHINNG
Lala: Has Grown. Her Hair.

HYUUU
ZHTT ZHTT
KYUU
IT'S HIM!!
ZZ
GATCH
RATTLE
RATTLE
RATTLE
?
GRRN
WHA-?!
YOU MUSTN'T TOUCH CERTAIN THINGS! IT PUTS YOU IN DANGER!
UH... UM...
IS THAT HOW YOU SEE WHAT HE DID?!
HUMPH! GO AWAY NOW!
A-ARE YOU OKAY...?
I-I'M FINE! I'M FINE.
SEE YOU.
AH! YOU DON'T...
IF ICHIJÔ HADN'T SAVED ME...
DOJI; DOJI; DOJI; DOJI-BIRON! ♫

Lala: Aggressive in Thought and in Love.

MIKO-CHIN! TAKE HER DOWN WITH YOUR SUPER KICK!
TAKE THAT AIRHEAD OUT WITH ONE SHOT!!
SHE'S NO MATCH FOR YOU!
POIT
NO! WHAT ARE YOU TALKING ABOUT?!
I'VE GOT NOTHING TO DO WITH THIS!
GWM GWM
WHAT?
NO MATCH FOR ME?
TWIK
HUMPH! THAT TYPE IS IN EVERY COUNTRY.
THE TRASH MAN AND SNEAK-THIEF WOMAN.
SKRRT
L-LALA-SAN!
SNEAK-THIEF WOMAN?
WHEN HAVE I STOLEN ANY-THING?
ZING
MY PAPA GOT WEAK WILL FROM WOMEN!
WHEN I SEE TRASH, I GET ANNOYED!
AH...!
SST
GRUNCH
YOU WANT TO FIGHT ME?
MIKOCHIN?
NO. I'M GOOD.
PLIP
PLIP
I WAS SAVING THAT APPLE FOR LAST.
JUST YOU WAIT!!
EVEN I CAN DO SOME-THING LIKE THAT!
......!!

むにゅっ
GLOOSH
BANANA.
OW! OW! OW! OWWW!
YOU'RE BREAKING ME!
GRIK
GRIK
GRIK
OOOOH!!
IRON CLAW!
SHE LIFTED IMADORI WITH ONE HAND! AMAZING STRENGTH!
I'M SORRY!!
YOU THINK HE'LL BE OKAY?
FORGET HIM.
LEAVE THIS TO ME!!
TMP
TAP
TAP
ポポンッ
BWAAM
?
DUWA!
VSH
DUUWA!!
DO YOU REMEMBER ME? DO YOU?
THE MASK! REMEMBER?

Tenma: This Makes Two Defeats.

WHA- ?!
SHUSSH
H-HARRY MCKENZIE?!
H-HE'S FROM THIS SCHOOL?!
I MEAN, HE'S HIGH-SCHOOL AGE?
YO.
N-NOT ONLY DID HE STEAL MY LINE, FEEL THAT PRESENCE!!
UHH... MY POSITION AS A CLASS REP WILL FALL...
OH! IT YOU...
......!!
YOU KNOW HIM, HARRY?
HA HA... IN WAY OF SPEAKING.
IT SEEMS OUR FATES CROSS IN MANY WAYS...
THAT MAKES IT INTEREST-ING!
I, TÔGÔ MASAKAZU, REPRESENT-ATIVE OF CLASS 2-D, WILL MAKE A PRO-POSAL!
LET US RESOLVE ALL OF CLASS 2-D AND 2-C'S DESTINIES AT THE UPCOMING ATHLETICS FAIR! WHAT DO YOU THINK?!
EH?!
WHOOAH!
OH, HO.
Sunglasses: Not This Time.

If It Were About Handsome Men, 2-C Has Lost Already.
H-HOW CAN YOU SAY THAT?!
AGAIN!! YOU STOLE THE LINE I WAS GOING TO SAY!!
AND YOU LOOKED SO COOL DOING IT!!
CHATTER CHATTER
WH-WHY DOES IT TURN OUT THAT WAY?!
I DON'T UNDERSTAND IT!!
DON'T GIVE US THAT!!
WE'LL DO IT!!
SOUNDS LIKE A GOOD IDEA TO ME!!
YEAH!!
BUT DON'T DECIDE FOR US!
CHATTER
HAS ICHIJŌ EVER MADE DECISIVE STATEMENTS LIKE THAT? I WONDER WHAT HAPPENED?
CHATTER
THEY'RE KIND OF COOL.
WHUMP
YOU DID NOT FIGHT HERE. THAT IS COWARDLY...
MIKO-CHIN!
SHTT
......
THUMP
YOU IDIOTS! GET OUTTA HERE!
WHAT WAS THAT SUP-POSED TO BE?!
QUIT TRYING TO PLAY US FOR FOOLS!!
JUST BECAUSE YOU'RE GOOD LOOKING!

FOR PITY'S SAKE!
SENSEI WARNED US NOT TO MAKE TROUBLE.
YOU'RE AS UNMANAGEABLE AS YOUR REPUTATION SUGGESTS.
HUMPH!
THEY ARE ONLY TALK!
HA...
EVEN THIS ONE...?
SST
WHAT?
TH-
THESE MARKS ARE...!!
I SEE... HA HA! I LOOK FORWARD TO THIS ATHLETICS FAIR, OR WHATEVER IT IS CALLED.
MIKOCHIN!!
......
YOU HAVE ONE MORE.
?
WHAT?!
B-BANANA?!
BANANA.
I-IT'S ALL OVER FOR ME...
WHAT'S HER SIZE?
A-ABOUT THE SAME SIZE AS MIKO-CHIN...
GOOD WORK!
KH...
I WILL KILL HIM!
YOU REALLY ARE A MAN!
THAT MAN WAS GOOD!
TWTCH
TWTCH

"Mikochin" Is Not Anyone's Name.

#71 . . . . Fin

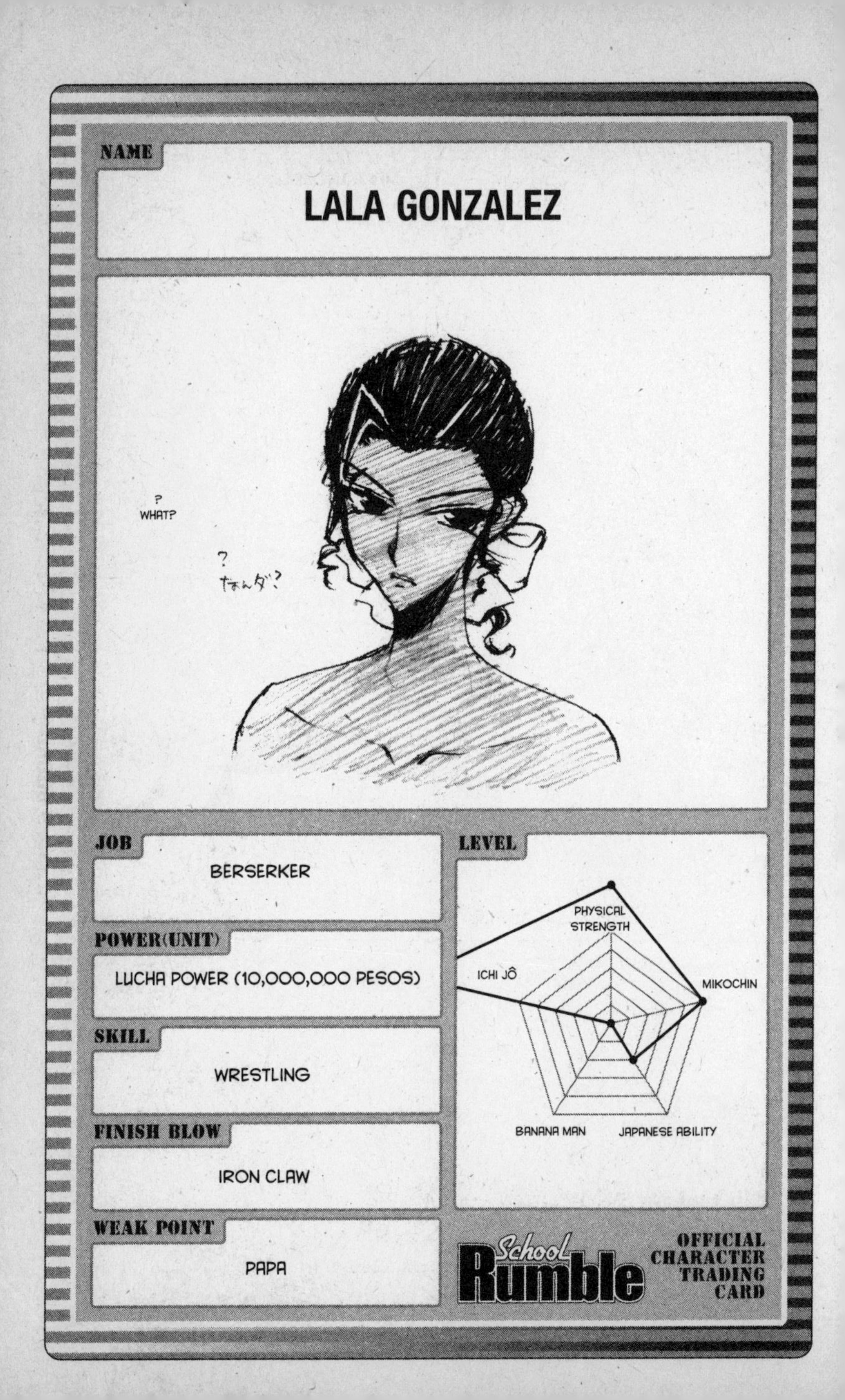
NAME
LALA GONZALEZ
?
WHAT?
?
なんダ?
JOB
BERSERKER
POWER(UNIT)
LUCHA POWER (10,000,000 PESOS)
SKILL
WRESTLING
FINISH BLOW
IRON CLAW
WEAK POINT
PAPA
LEVEL
PHYSICAL STRENGTH
MIKOCHIN
JAPANESE ABILITY
BANANA MAN
ICHI JÔ
School Rumble
OFFICIAL CHARACTER TRADING CARD

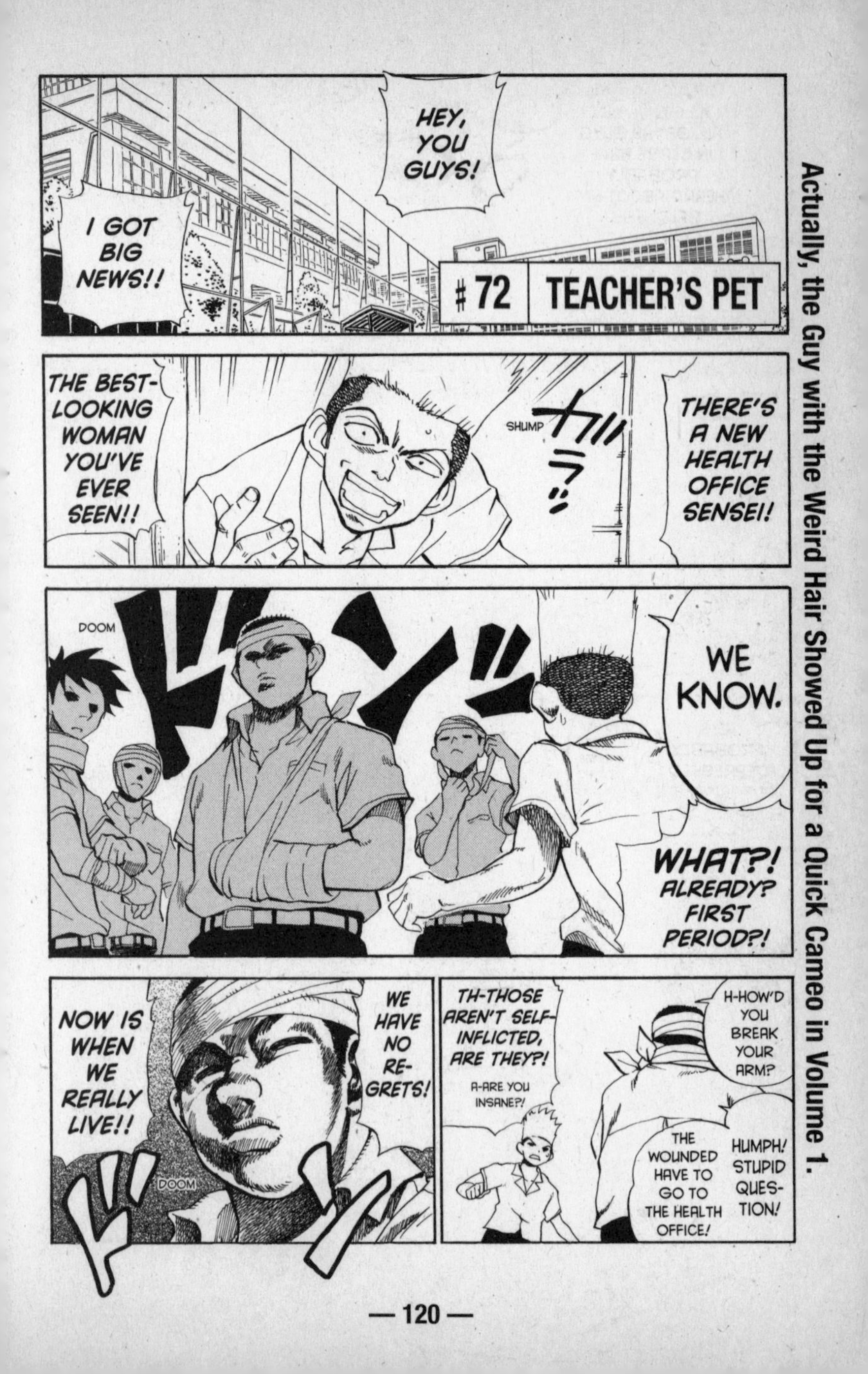
HEY, YOU GUYS!
I GOT BIG NEWS!!
72 TEACHER'S PET
THERE'S A NEW HEALTH OFFICE SENSEI!
SHUMP
THE BEST-LOOKING WOMAN YOU'VE EVER SEEN!!
WE KNOW.
WHAT?! ALREADY? FIRST PERIOD?!
DOOM
H-HOW'D YOU BREAK YOUR ARM?
HUMPH! STUPID QUES-TION!
THE WOUNDED HAVE TO GO TO THE HEALTH OFFICE!
TH-THOSE AREN'T SELF-INFLICTED, ARE THEY?!
A-ARE YOU INSANE?!
WE HAVE NO RE-GRETS!
NOW IS WHEN WE REALLY LIVE!!
DOOM
Actually, the Guy with the Weird Hair Showed Up for a Quick Cameo in Volume 1.

Nishimoto Is Also a Veteran of Volume 1.

Sawachika Eri: Understands It's Her Fault, but...
WHAT!
I JUST THOUGHT THAT MAYBE YOU SHOULD APOLOGIZE.
WHY?! I APOLOGIZED BEFORE!!
AND THEN YOU DID SOMETHING WORSE.
HEY, JUST APOLOGIZE ONCE MORE, AND ALL'S HEALED!
AND THAT'LL END IT.
NEVER! NEVER, EVER!!
SKRK
LOOK AT THE SELFISH RICH GIRL!!
REAL BEAUTY DOES WHAT'S RIGHT.
GAK!
THAT'S RIGHT, ERI-CHAN! APOLOGIZE!
URK!
.... !!
OKAY, FINE!!!
WHATEVER YOU WANT!!
TAK
TAK
HEY, YOU THERE!
Y--
YES!
HAVE YOU SEEN HARIMA-KUN? WHERE IS HE?
......
THERE'S SOMETHING FUNDAMENTALLY DIFFERENT FROM US.
WHEN IT COMES TO ERI.
HARIMA IS IN THE HEALTH OFFICE.
P-PROBABLY.
REALLY? THANK YOU!
YES!

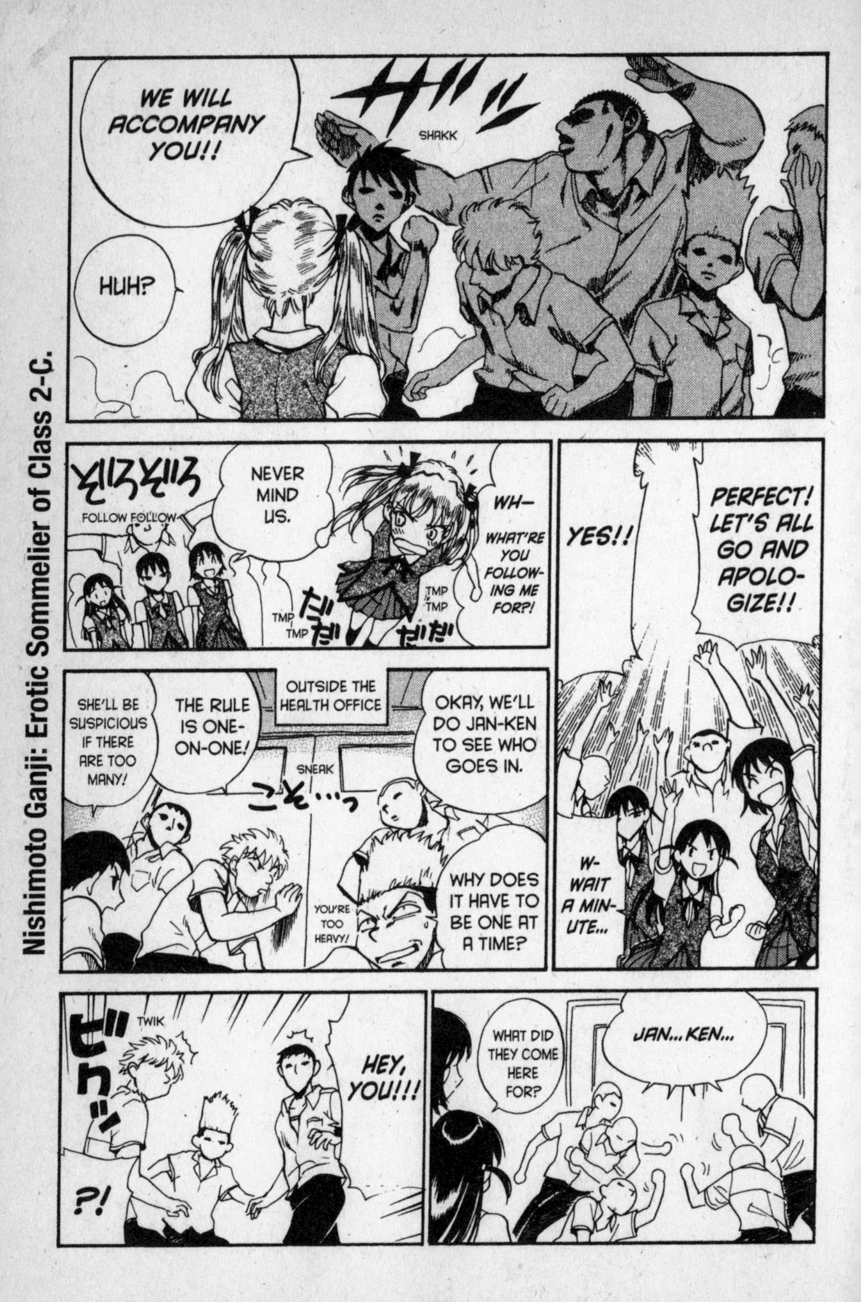

WE WILL ACCOMPANY YOU!!
SHAKK
HUH?
PERFECT! LET'S ALL GO AND APOLO-GIZE!!
YES!!
W-WAIT A MIN-UTE...
WH— WHAT'RE YOU FOLLOW-ING ME FOR?!
NEVER MIND US.
FOLLOW FOLLOW
TMP TMP
TMP TMP
OUTSIDE THE HEALTH OFFICE
OKAY, WE'LL DO JAN-KEN TO SEE WHO GOES IN.
THE RULE IS ONE-ON-ONE!
SHE'LL BE SUSPICIOUS IF THERE ARE TOO MANY!
SNEAK
WHY DOES IT HAVE TO BE ONE AT A TIME?
YOU'RE TOO HEAVY!
JAN...KEN...
WHAT DID THEY COME HERE FOR?
HEY, YOU!!!
TWIK
?!
Nishimoto Ganji: Erotic Sommelier of Class 2-C.

IT'S YOU GUYS AGAIN!
I KEEP TELLING YOU NOT TO MAKE NOISE IN THE HALL!!
STOMP STOMP STOMP
GAK!!
IT'S THE GUIDANCE COUNSELOR, GORIYAMA!!
L-LET'S GET OUTTA HERE!!
TMP
WHY DO WE HAVE TO RUN AWAY?!
I-I DON'T KNOW, BUT RUN ANY-WAY!!
ONE! TWO! THREE!!
VWISH
ARE YOU GUYS NINJA OR SOME-THING?!
EH?
WHAT?
WHAT'S GOING ON?
GLOOM
COME WITH ME!
EHH?! BUT WHY?!
THUMP
THUMP
TSUKA-MOTO!!
LEAVE TENMA TO ME.
I'LL GET HER BACK.
THE GUY'S A DIM-WIT.
EVERYONE SCATTERED IN ALL DIREC-TIONS.
THAT MAKES IT PERFECT!

A NEW HEALTH OFFICE SENSEI...?
OH YEAH! I HEARD THEY WERE SUPPOSED TO GET A NEW ONE AT THE START OF THE SECOND SEMESTER.
SHE ARRIVED A LITTLE LATE, BUT...
THE LAST ONE WAS A NICE LADY, THOUGH...
HMM...
I DON'T WANT ANYBODY TO SEE ME APOLOGIZE TO HIM.
WHO CARES? JUST GET IN THERE!
Health Office
I-I KNOW!!
KLIK
KLIK
KLIK
ZZZ
ZZZ
MM...
MMMM...
TENMA-CHAN, MUMBLE MUMBLE...
もぞりっ...
SHUCH
キィッ
SRSHH
TONK
AH!
I LEFT THE WINDOW ABOVE THE BED OPEN.
OH! THERE'S A KID SLEEPING HERE.
カラカラッ
SHUUMP
MMM...

EH?
That Girl...
ZZZZ
ZZZZ
HMM...
.....
じーっ
STARE
!
ぽむっ
POFF

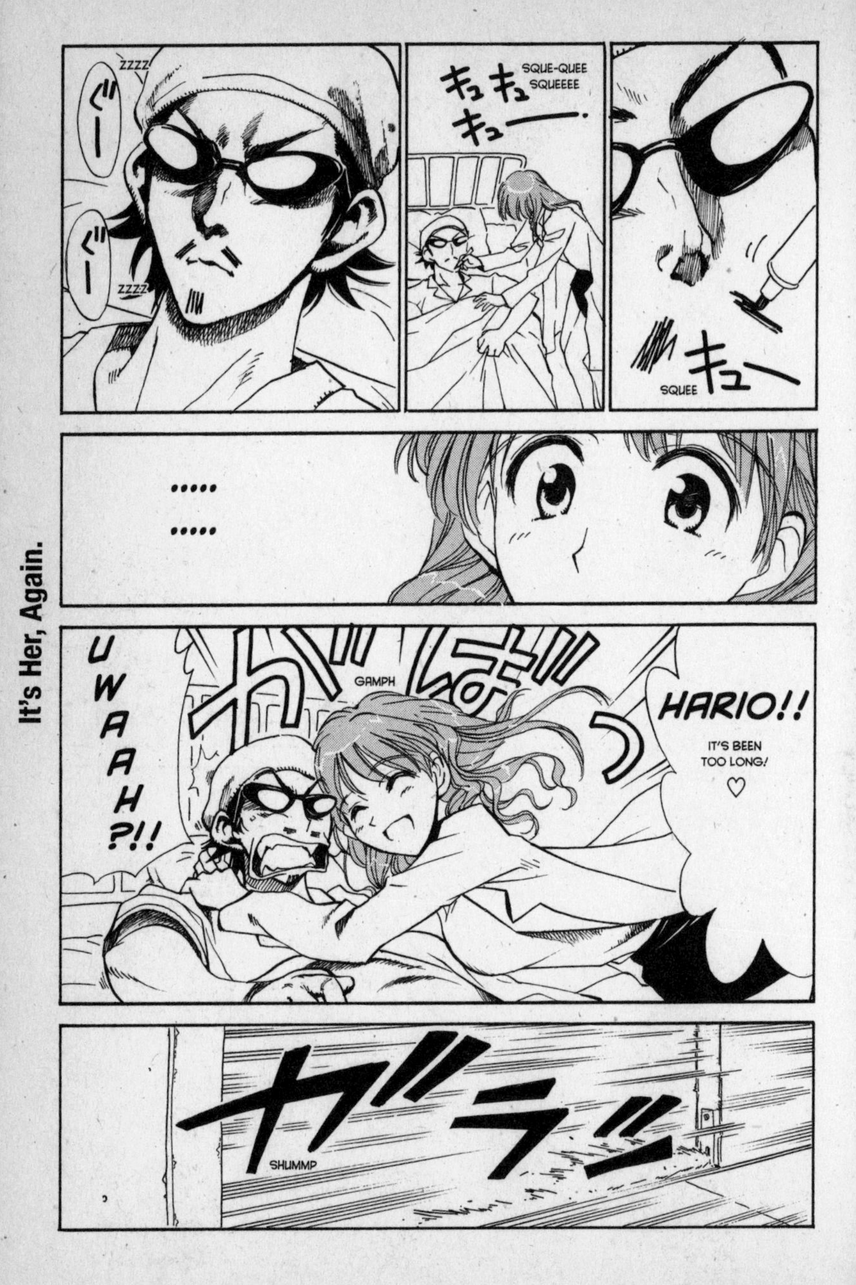
キュー
SQUEE
キュキュキュー
SQUE-QUEE SQUEEEE
ぐー
ZZZZ
ぐー
ZZZZ
.....
.....
HARIO!!
IT'S BEEN TOO LONG! ♡
GAMPH
UWAAH?!!
SHUMMP

No Shining Wizard Here.

72· · · · · · · · ·Fin

The ♭ Stories Are Like the Main Story's B-Side, and They're Unlike It, Too.
I'VE GOT WORK NOW.
SEE YOU, YAKUMO!
VRRM
BEE-BEEP
YEAH. SEE YOU.
CHINESE RESTAURANT
GOOD MORNING!
KARANG
HUH? WHAT'S WRONG, CHIN-TENCHÔ?
AH, SARAH, SOME-THING HAS HAP-PENED!!
YOU SEE, A FRIEND CALLED TO SAY MY WIFE IS IN LABOR!
IT IS A WEEK EARLY, BUT SHE WILL HAVE HER BABY!
YOU SHOULD GO TO HER.
BUT... PEOPLE MADE RESERVA-TIONS...
AND ONE PERSON EACH IN THE KITCHEN AND ON THE FLOOR ARE OUT TODAY.
THE ONLY THING TO DO IS CLOSE UP!
♭13 CHINA GIRL

JUST LEAVE THE RESTAURANT TO US!
AND I'M SURE YOUR WIFE NEEDS YOU NOW.
THANK YOU!!
SORRY, YOU TWO!
I WILL SEE YOU!
WE SHOULD REALLY JUST CLOSE UP.
AT LEAST WE SHOULD SERVE THE CUSTOMERS WHO HAVE RESERVATIONS.
THE TWO OF US CAN'T HANDLE THIS ALONE.
ALL WE HAVE TO DO IS EXPLAIN IT TO THEM.
你好!!
(HELLO!)
陳老弟,好久不見,好嗎?
(HEY CHIN, LONG TIME NO SEE! HOW'VE YOU BEEN?)
8个人,来干活的!!
(8 OF US! WE'LL MAKE YOU WORK TODAY!)
SHUFFLE SHUFFLE
URK!
Sarah: Asô's Kôhai by One Year.

肚子饿了！
(OH, I'M HUNGRY!)
老板！来杯水！
(BOSS! FIRST LET'S GET SOME ICE WATER HERE!)
SLUMP SLUMP
UH...I'M VERY SORRY, BUT THE OWNER IS TAKING THE DAY OFF TODAY...
HEY, DO YOU KNOW CHINESE?
I CAN'T GET THROUGH TO THEM.
NOT AT ALL.
ENGLISH MAYBE, BUT...
AND IT'D BE RUDE TO FORCE THEM TO LEAVE.
LET'S GIVE IT A TRY.
ARE YOU STUPID! ALL THESE PEOPLE?!
BUT... THEY SEEM TO BE HAVING SO MUCH FUN...
THEY'RE ALREADY STARTING
乾杯
KAMPAI!
KLINK
KLINK
URK!
THOSE GUYS...
I'LL WORK IN THE KITCHEN.
I MAY NOT LOOK IT, BUT I'M A GOOD COOK.
ALL THE PREPARATIONS ARE DONE, SO I ONLY HAVE TO WORK ON THE MENU ITEMS.
SEMPAI, IF YOU COULD TAKE THE ORDERS...
WE'LL BE FINE!

HERE!
ONE HAPPÔSAI VEGETABLE STIR-FRY!
I BROUGHT YOUR HAPPÔSAI.
哈!哈!哈!
(HA!) (HA!) (HA!)
SHASHH
Flip!
ADD IN A SHRIMP IN CHILE SAUCE.
GOT IT!
.....
.....
THE GUYS SEEM PRETTY HAPPY ABOUT EVERYTHING.
OH, REALLY? I'M GLAD!
HA HA...
SHE'S WEIRD.
HM?
カラカラン
DING DING
HEY!! HOW MANY ARE SUPPOSED TO COME?
THERE'S MORE?!
どやどや
MURMUR MURMUR

Asô Hiroyoshi: In the Same Class as Tenma.

SHUSSH
W-WOW!
DIDN'T I EVER TELL YOU? MY FAMILY OWNS A RAMEN SHOP.
HUP!
CHAA
CHAA
FIRST I'VE HEARD OF IT!
REALLY!!
HEY! THE ORDERS!
AH! O-OKAY!
CHASH
OH, ONE MORE THING.
YES?
DON'T OVERDO IT.
HUUUH?
YOU'VE GOT A NICE SIDE, TOO.
KARANG
OWCH!!
DO YOUR BEST!
ZWOOM ZWOOM

味道不错小姐！
(THAT WAS GOOD, YOUNG LADY!)
TROMP TROMP
THANK YOU SO MUCH!
?
HEY! ADD ON SOME BOILED GYOZA, OKAY?
わいわい
CHATTER CHATTER
OKAY, THANKS FOR WAITING!
THAT WAS GOOD! BETTER THAN USUAL TODAY.
THANK YOU SO MUCH!
SO THE SHOP'S BEEN TAKEN OVER BY A YOUNG MARRIED COUPLE, HUH? FINE WITH ME!
PEACE! PEACE!
AH HA HA HA HA!
THAT IS SO WRONG!
COMPLETELY!
きっぱり
Closed.
A JOB WELL DONE!!
SLAPP
GOOD JOB.
AHH! I'M WORN OUT!
WHUMP
I'VE NEVER CURSED THE DAY THAT I'M FROM A RAMEN SHOP FAMILY LIKE I DO TODAY!
?
TONK
THANK YOU SO MUCH FOR TODAY!
YOU HAVEN'T EATEN YET, RIGHT?
I FORCED YOU INTO IT.

Sarah and Asô: One Delicious Couple.

♭13· · · · · · · · · ·Fin

♭14 PICTURE PERFECT
Faculty
After a Long Time, Sasakura-sensei.
SO PLEASE PREPARE THE AV ROOM, OKAY?
SORRY TO PUT YOU OUT.
JUST BECAUSE YOU'RE IN A FRONT SEAT.
I'LL DO IT.
HERE ARE THE PRINT-OUTS YOU WANTED.
OH! THANK YOU.
SQUEE
IT MUST BE ROUGH ON YOU, TSUKAMOTO-SAN.
YOU WERE SENT ON ANOTHER ERRAND?
AH!
NO, I JUST...
ORDERS FROM THE COUNSELORS AND YOUR CLASS. YOU'VE RUN OUT OF LUCK, HUH?
IF YOU'LL EXCUSE ME...
SAY HELLO TO SARAH FOR ME.
SHE'S A NICE GIRL, HUH?
"THEY DON'T MAKE 'EM LIKE THAT ANYMORE."
THAT'S THE TYPE SHE IS.
QUITE DIFFERENT FROM HOW YOU WERE, OSAKABE-SENSEI.
WE AGREED TO FORGET THAT...
I'M JUST JOKING. YOU'VE TURNED INTO A FINE TEACHER.
HA HA HA...
THAT'S RIGHT.
IF I'M GOOD NOW, IT'S ALL THAT MATTERS.

Sasakura-sensei: Unexpectedly Good at Bargaining.
AH!
BY THE WAY, ABOUT BEING A MODEL...
...DID YOU CONSIDER THE OFFER?
OH, NO!
I KNEW YOU'D ASK!
ALL RIGHT. I'LL DO IT.
WHAT WOULD YOU SAY IF I TURNED YOU DOWN?
THANK YOU SO MUCH!
わい
CHATTER
2-C
わい
CHATTER
HWOOOHH!!
GO!! GO!! GO!!
NNGGGH!
JUST WHAT THE ODDS SAID WOULD HAPPEN!!
DON'T GIVE ME THAT!!
SHUMP
がらっ
HEY!
YOU'RE IN IT NOW! WITH THE LUNCHES YOU'VE BET, YOU'D BETTER START FASTING!
STOP IT!!
WE HAVE A NEW TOPIC.
SLOOP
ぼそっ
TWIK
TMP
TMP
......
SKRRT SKRT
SKRRT SKRT
WH-WHAT?
THEY'RE LINING UP THEIR DESKS.
WHAT'S GOING ON?

OKAY THEN. WHAT IS IT TODAY?
HUSSSSH
GULP
SHH!
SASAKURA-SENSEI WILL BE PUTTING ON AN EXHIBITION. AND THE MODEL FOR ONE OF THE PAINTINGS TO BE UNVEILED HAS BEEN DECIDED TODAY.
ACCORDING TO THE INFORMATION I HAVE BEEN ABLE TO OBTAIN, THE MODEL FOR THIS NUDE PAINTING WILL BE OSAKABE ITOKO-SENSEI.
YOU SEE?
HUH?!
EH?!
YOU'RE KID-
URK!
IT MAY JUST BE A PAINTING, BUT I WILL WORSHIP THE BEAUTIFUL BODY OF ITOKO-SENSEI!!!!
THOSE SEDUCTIVE CURVES EVEN NOW FLOAT BEFORE MY EYES!
DAAAAH!!
DAMN, NISHIMOTO'S INFORMATION IS INVALUABLE!!
UWAAAAH!!
GULP
AAH!! HE IS THE CLASS'S NO. 1 EROS SOMMELIER!!!
THAT'S WHAT A MAN BORN INTO A VIDEO SHOP FAMILY CAN DO!!!
NISHIMOTO GANJI. 17 YEARS OLD.
THE COMBINATION OF HIS MILD MANNERS AND HIS REPUTATION FOR MINISTERING TO THE HOPES OF THE MEN OF CLASS 2-C HAS MADE HIM KNOWN AND LOVED AS BUDDHA NISHIMOTO.
QUOTED FROM THE "DAINISHIDEN."
PLEASE, SETTLE DOWN.
IMADORI, WHAT IS SENSEI'S SIZE?
NO DOUBT ABOUT IT.
IT'S D!!
ZHING
WHOA!
I KNEW IT!
IMADORI KYŌSUKE (HUMMINGBIRD) ONE OF THE FIVE TIGER GENERALS. PLEDGED TO BE A BLOOD BROTHER WITH NISHIMOTO. THIS "VIDEO STORE VOW" HAS GAINED FAME THROUGHOUT THE LAND.

Why Are You Worried, Hanai?
ITOKO-SENSEI AS SOURCE MATERIAL! ♬
THE TOP-SECRET KIND! ♡
NARA-CCHI! HELP ME WITH DISTRIBU-TION!
AH... SURE!
NARA KENTARÔ, MINION.
Fuyuki Takeichi (The White Egret). Hoping to add Fuyuki's intelligence-gathering abilities, Nishimoto approached him with the video "Three Visitations."
OOH!! TH-THIS IS...
WOW!
ざわ…!
CHATTER
THEY'RE IDIOTS.
SOMEHOW WE ENDED UP WITH A LOT OF USELESS GUYS IN OUR CLASS.
COMPLETELY TRANSFIXED BY SKIRTS.
BUT AREN'T YOU A LITTLE WORRIED WHEN THEY TALK ABOUT ITOKO-SENSEI BEING NUDE?
AH! YOU TOO?
SHE DOES HAVE A GOOD BODY, HUH?
IT'S ALMOST A SHAME SHE'S A TEACHER.
URRG!!
WHAT'LL I DO?
LOOK! LOOK!
HE'S WORRIED ABOUT IT!
HARIMA-KUN DOESN'T SEEM FAZED BY IT.
KLIKA
KLIKA
2-C
THE SUPER-MASSIVE ASTRONOM-ICAL OBJECT A BENDS THE LIGHT OF OBJECT B SO THAT TWO IMAGES CAN BE SEEN.
WHAT DO YOU THINK OF THAT?
B
A
P
カッ
KAK
......
カリカリ カリカリ
SKRTCH SKRTCH SKRTCH SKRTCH
もくもく もくもく
SHUFFLE SHUFFLE SHUFFLE SHUFFLE
....
SKRTCH SKRTCH SKRTCH SKRTCH
カリカリカリ カリカリカリカ
もくもくもくもく
SHUFFLE SHUFFLE SHUFFLE SHUFFLE
......
YOUR CON-CENTRATION IS SUDDENLY GOOD TODAY.
DON'T GIVE YOUR-SELVES ULCERS.
SKRTCH SKRTCH SKRTCH SKRTCH SKRTCH SKRTCH
SKRTCH SKRTCH SKRTCH SKRTCH SKRTCH SKRTCH

HEE HEH HO HEH
ヒヘホへ
EH HEH HEH
NIIIICE...
I CAN'T BEAT THAT!
HEE HA HA HO
コンッ
THOK
OW!
"NO, NO! SEND IT ONE PERSON FARTHER"...?
?
はのだ
TWINK PINK
WHAT? A LETTER?
.....!!
SHFF SHFF
THAT THING ABOUT HER BEING A MODEL! HOW CAN I ASK HER? IT'S DRIVING ME NUTS!!
?
トトン
TAP TAP
HERE.
SLUMP
I DON'T WANT TO LIVE ANY-MORE!
EH? .....
INNOCENT BYSTANDER.
NO REACTION. (PRESSURE OF SILENCE.)
TOMORROW HE IS CERTAIN TO BE HELD IN PUBLIC RIDICULE AMONG THE GIRLS.
SKRITCH SKRITCH
Cafeteria
わいわい
CHATTER CHATTER
SLRRP SLRRP
ズズー
カチャ
KACHAK
WHISPER.
THE EXHIBITION'S OPENING HAS BEEN LOCKED IN. NEXT WEEK ON SATURDAY. ADJUST ACCORDINGLY.
ROGER. CONSIDER MY DATE CANCELED.
ちゅるん
ZLUU-ZLUUP

Apparently Much Has Gone on Between Them.

SEVERAL DAYS LATER...
2-C
GOT IT. GOOD WORK.
GRRK
GULP
ON SATURDAY THIS WEEK...
WE'RE GOING IN!!
YAAAAH!!
Yaah!
BUT IT'S STILL JUST A PAINTING...
SOMEONE WISE ONCE SAID THAT WE HAVE EYES WITHIN OUR HEARTS.
絵画展
笹倉葉子
YOHKO SASAKURA
ON THE FATEFUL DAY...
LET THE BATTLE BEGIN!!
ZZHH
DOGONG
ATTACK!!
HYAAAAAHH!!!
DM DM DM DM DM DM DM DM DM
ITOKO-SAAAN!
WAIT FOR MEEE! ♡

<CUBISM>
Ahh, the Sunset Pierces One's Eyes.
OOOHHH...
サァァー
PILLARS OF SALT.
SASAKURA-SENSEI, CONGRATULATIONS ON YOUR EXHIBITION.
THANK YOU!
イヤァァァ...
NOOOO!
WOW!
CRUMBLE CRUMBLE
ボロボロ
OH, BOY!
HM?
SST
ス...
.... HUMPH....
I THOUGHT IT WOULD TURN OUT THIS WAY.
I JUST CAME TO KEEP WATCH OVER YOU GUYS.
だだだ
TMP TMP TMP
LET'S GO HOME.
I DON'T QUITE UNDERSTAND IT, BUT OSAKABE-SENSEI ONCE SAID THE FOLLOWING...
YES, BACK THEN AND NOW, MEN WILL NEVER CHANGE. (YAKUMO)

♭14·········Fin

MY NAME IS LALA.
I LIVE ALONE WITH MY LUCHADOR FATHER IN MY MOTHERLAND, MEXICO.
♭15 ONCE UPON A TIME IN MEXICO
KACHAK
FATHER!
DID YOU LOSE AGAIN?!
UMM...
TMP
I TOLD YOU TO GIVE UP THE BOOZE!
WE DON'T HAVE ANY MORE MONEY!
UN...
C... CAREN...
WHEN MY FATHER IS DRUNK, HE ALWAYS MUTTERS MY MOTHER'S NAME...
FATHER STILL LOVES HER...
THE ONLY THING MY FATHER EVER DID FOR ME WAS ONE THING...
EVER SINCE I WAS VERY YOUNG, HE DRUMMED ALL THE TRICKS OF LUCHA INTO MY HEAD.

LUCHA: ITS REAL NAME IS LUCHA LIBRE, THE SPORT OF PROFESSIONAL WRESTLING IN MEXICO.

LOOK THERE, LALA...
BEYOND THE SUN THERE IS A LAND CALLED JAPÔN.
IT IS A RICH LAND THAT HAS EVERY-THING.
LET'S WORK HARD AND SAVE MONEY, AND THAT WAY WE'LL BOTH GO TO JAPÔN!
ONCE WE'RE RICH, MAMA IS SURE TO COME BACK TO US!
YEAH!
...LEZ!
GONZALEZ!
WHOOSH
WHAT, ARE YOU ASLEEP DOWN THERE?
IT'S TIME FOR YOUR MATCH!!
FOR PITY'S SAKE! I KNOW THAT THE ONE YOU'RE MATCHED AGAINST IS NOBODY FAMOUS, BUT...
...DURING A PRACTICE MATCH, SHE TOOK DOWN MIURA!
AND IN ONLY 5 SECONDS!
YOU DON'T KNOW HOW MUCH STRENGTH YOU HAVE! WHEN YOU'RE DOWN AND NEARLY OUT, IT CAN SAVE YOU!
MANAGER...

ARE YOU SAYING I MAY LOSE?
TWITCH
....!!
GAH...
G-GET GOING!!
YES...
SST
I DON'T CARE WHO MY OPPONENT IS, I WILL NEVER LOSE!
DUWA!
にく
SH- SHE'S A...
...LUCHA-DOR?!
JAPONESE... ARE YOU TRYING TO INSULT ME?
NO MATTER!
THIS'LL TAKE ONE SECOND!!

YEAH... YOU WON WITH ENERGY TO SPARE!

THAT'S MY GONZ! I'M EXPECTING BIG THINGS FROM YOU IN THE MATCHES TO COME!

IF OUR SCHOOL BACKS US UP, WE COULD TAKE THE INTER-HIGH CHAMPION-SHIP!

IT'S JUST WHAT YOUR FATHER BACK HOME WANTED! HA HA HA!

YES, MANAGER...

YES...

I STILL DON'T GET WHAT THE DEAL WAS WITH THAT GIRL I WRESTLED.

IT'S LIKE SHE HAD NO EXPER-IENCE AT ALL!

HER MASK WAS UGLY, TOO.

S-STOP RIGHT THERE!!

HM?

A FIGHT? THERE ARE VIOLENT PEOPLE IN JAPÔN AS WELL.

WHA-?!

The Markings on the Mask Are Different from Tenma's, but...

So, This Happened Offscreen During Chapter # 61?!
SIGH...
WH- WHAT'S THIS?
A DELICATE LITTLE GIRL HAS THAT KIND OF STRENGTH?!
I-ICHI JÔ!!
EH?
IT IS HER! IT'S ICHI JÔ! THE ONE I DEFEATED TODAY!
SHF
SHEEN
UM...
U-UH...
WHO MIGHT YOU BE?
WHY?!
WHY YOU NOT GIVE YOUR ALL?
UM... UM... EH...?
DMP
AN-SWER ME!!

TMP
WHOOSH
?!
KYUUN
WHOOSH
KH?!
WH—
SH-
SHE VAN-ISHED?!
UFF?!
GAMPH
SH-SHE'S REALLY...
IMPOSSIBLE!
WH-WHEN COULD SHE HAVE...

...GOOD!!
A-ARE YOU ALL RIGHT?!
I'M SORRY! I'M SO SORRY!
MY BODY JUST REACTED!
WHAT IS THIS GIRL?!
YOU... WHAT IS YOUR NAME...?
EH...?
UM... MY NAME IS I-ICHIJÔ KAREN...
WHAT...?!
C-CAREN?!
IT MUST BE A JOKE PLAYED ON ME BY GOD.
I NEVER THOUGHT I'D HEAR MY MOTHER'S NAME MENTIONED IN SUCH A FAR-OFF COUNTRY...
AND LATER...
ICHI-JÔ! YOU EAT LUNCH WITH ME!
TRANS-FERRED TO THE NEXT CLASS-ROOM OVER.

Ichijô Karen: The Legend of Her Skill Begins.

♭15· · · · · · · · ·Fin

CLASS 2-C, UMEZU SHIGEO, 17 YEARS OLD, MEMBER OF THE TRACK & FIELD CLUB. HIS LOOKS ARE CONSIDERED MORE OR LESS FRESH-FACED. (ACCORDING TO THE GIRLS.)
THERE IS A GIRL HE HAS RECENTLY STARTED DATING.
KIDO MADOKA, ALSO IN THE TRACK & FIELD CLUB.
IT'S A COMMON STORY, BUT ACCORDING TO RUMORS, EVENTS HAPPENED BETWEEN THEM DURING SUMMER VACATION, AND THEY STARTED DATING. (DETAILS OMITTED.)
SINCE THEY ARE IN THE SAME CLUB, IT CAN'T BE CONSIDERED COMPLETELY UNEXPECTED.
BUT TO LISTEN TO THE PEOPLE AROUND THEM, THEY WERE SURPRISED AT THE DEVELOPMENT.
THAT'S HOW IT GOES.
BECAUSE IT WAS SUMMER VACATION, THEIR DATES WERE FULL AND SATISFYING.
THEY DID A LOT OF PREPARATION FOR THE DATES, BUT IN THE END, WENT WITH THE FLOW.
AS A COUPLE, THEIR RELATIONSHIP SEEMED AS STRONG AS EVER.
YAAY YAAY
NOW THIS ATHLETICS FAIR HAS REALLY HEATED UP!!
YAAY YAAY
IT SEEMED THEY HAD A GOOD, STRONG START, BUT...
...HE HAD ONE OVERRIDING WORRY.
♭16 RUNNING MAN

I CAN'T...
...KISS HER!!
WHAT A DISASTER!
I KEEP LOOKING FOR THE NEXT CHANCE TO COME ALONG...
...BUT I LET EVERY ONE PASS ME BY!!
I JUST DON'T HAVE ANY COURAGE!!
THERE'S THIS TIME...
SEE YA!
OH, THAT TIME TOO!!!
THAT TIME...
CHRRP
CHRRP
ANYBODY NORMAL WOULD HAVE KISSED HER THEN!!
SO FAR, MADOKA HASN'T ACTED SUSPICIOUS, BUT...
I CAN'T HELP BUT THINK THAT SHE'S DISAPPOINTED AT HOW IMMATURE I AM!
SORRY, MADOKA...!
BUT—!!
GRATCH
TODAY AT THE ATHLETICS FAIR...
...FOR SOME REASON THE PEOPLE IN MY CLASS ARE ACTING WEIRD!
GWMM
B-BMP
B-BMP
B-BMP
THIS IS A CHANCE I COULDN'T EVEN HAVE WISHED FOR! I'LL SHOW HER MY BEST SIDE, AND IN THE EXCITEMENT, I'LL TAKE MADOKA AND...

WE'RE DEFINITELY GOING TO DO THIS!!
KLNCH
YAAY
YAAY
WELL SAID, UMEZU!!
THIS IS HOW 2-C WILL WIN!!
I'LL BE CHEERING YOU WITH ALL MY STRENGTH!!
POFF
HUH?
YOU'VE GOT NOTHING TO DO WITH THIS.
THE 8TH HEAT OF THE 100 METER!
GLOOM
WHAT'S SO AWFUL ABOUT ME?!
UMEZU IS UP NEXT? WE'RE CHEERING FOR YOU!!
SET!!
GRN
RIGHT! I'M ON THE TRACK & FIELD TEAM! I CAN'T LOSE!
WATCH ME, MADOKA! I'M GOING TO WIN THIS!!
NO DOUBT ABOUT IT!!
BANG
I'M GOING TO...!
SKRCH SKR-SKRCH
SKRCH SKR-SKRCH
TMP

KISS YOU !!
BWEET BWEET
WHAT?! A PIG?!
A PIG JUST RAN ONTO THE TRACK!!
AND JUST AT THE MOMENT THEY STARTED RUNNING!!
CHATTER
SHIGEO WAS HIT BY A PIG IN A HIT-AND-RUN ACCI-DENT!!
WHAT...
WHAT'S A PIG EVEN DOING ON THE GROUNDS ANYWAY?!!

Pig.

Health Office
UNH...
AH!
GAMPH
AH! YOU'VE COME TO?
SENSEI!
I-I PASSED OUT?!
YOU HIT YOUR HEAD VERY HARD.
YOU WERE IN A TRACK AND FIELD DASH, HUH?
I WAS GOING ALL OUT WHEN I HIT THE PIG. ← TAKEN TO THE HEALTH OFFICE.
TH-THIS IS THE WORST...!!
UM... I HAVE TO GO NOW.
I NEED TO BE AT THE FAIR'S HEAD-QUARTERS.
KLAP
IT'S ALL OVER... MY KISS...
SO I LEAVE HIM TO YOU. ♡
OKAY.
POFF
AH!

Umezu Shigeo: A 17-Year-Old with Worries.

MADOKA...
ARE YOU ALL RIGHT, SHIGEO?
DAMMIT. THE WORDS JUST WON'T COME OUT!
SORRY, MADOKA.
THUMP
WHAT ARE YOU APOLOGIZING FOR? IT WAS A PIG. HOW COULD YOU AVOID IT?
I CAN'T TELL HER.
I'D SHOW HER MY BEST SIDE, AND IN THE EXCITEMENT...
...I'D KISS HER. THAT'S WHAT I WAS AIMING FOR.
GLANCE
I WAS REALLY WORRIED FOR YOU.
BUT I'M SO HAPPY THAT YOU'RE OKAY!
SMILE
GLEEM
PURIFIED IN HER LIGHT.
I HAVE THIS TERRIBLE FEELING THAT I'LL NEVER BE ABLE TO SEE MY OWN PLANS THROUGH!
THIS IS PATHETIC!
YOU DON'T HAVE TO BE SO DISAPPOINTED!
IT'S GOT YOU DOWN RIGHT NOW, BUT IT'LL BE OKAY!
THE TEAM WILL BOUNCE BACK!
THE GIRLS ARE GOOD!
SUÔ-SAN, SAWACHIKA-SAN, AND ALSO...
...I THINK THAT ICHIJÔ-SAN IS AMAZING.
NOBODY'S NOTICED HER YET, THOUGH.
GLBBA GLBBA

I GUESS I CAN WATCH THE RACES WITHOUT WORRY-ING.
NOT ONLY THAT. THEY'VE GOT YOU, TOO.
THANKS.
WE'LL GO ON TO WIN.
THAT'S WHY...
...I HAVE A FAVOR TO ASK OF YOU, SHIGEO.
HM?
IF I COME IN FIRST, I WANT MY PRIZE TO BE A KISS FROM YOU, OKAY?
SPRTZZ
KAFF! KAFF!
OH, NO! HEY! ARE YOU ALL RIGHT?
WAS IT TOO HOT?
SHE TAKES THE VERY THING I'M SO WORRIED ABOUT AND WITH THOUGHTLESS EASE...
AS IF IT WERE SOME BONUS CHOCOLATE TREAT.
TH-THAT CAN'T BE FOR-GIVEN!!
HON-ESTLY!
WELL? WHAT DO YOU THINK?
HUH?
KH...!
I DON'T KNOW ABOUT FEMALE HIGH SCHOOL STUDENTS THESE DAYS...!
B-BUT...
MADOKA, YOU'RE *CERTAIN* TO COME IN FIRST!
WHAT KIND OF PRIZE WOULD THAT BE?
NO! WHAT AM I SAYING?! MADOKA IS GIVING ME MY CHANCE, AND I'M GOING TO BLOW IT AGAIN?!

EH...?
WHA—
WHA-WHA-WHA-WHA-WHA-WHA?!
W—
WASN'T IT SUPPOSED TO BE A PRIZE?!
HEH, HEH...
THIS WAY IT'LL BE IMPOSSIBLE FOR ME TO LOSE!
AND YOU'RE THE REASON, SHIGEO.
WELL, IT'S MY TURN NOW...
I GOTTA GIVE IT MY ALL!
Y-YEAH...
I DON'T BELIEVE THAT WOMAN!
SHUUMP
WOMEN THESE DAYS!!
YAHOO!!
AT ABOUT THE SAME TIME...
N-NAPOLEON?!
WHY ARE YOU HERE?!
BWEET, BWEET.

So It Was Harima's Pig...

♭16·········Fin

IT'S COMING...

...JUNE 26, 2007!

2004.6
KC
MAGAZINE

About the Creator

Jin Kobayashi was born in Tokyo. *School Rumble* is his first manga series. He has answered these questions from his fans:

What is your hobby?
Basketball

Which manga inspired you to become a creator?
Dragon Ball

Which character in your manga do you like best?
Kenji Harima

What type of manga do you want to create in the future?
Action

Name one book, piece of music, or movie you like.
The Indiana Jones series

Translation Notes

Japanese is a tricky language for most Westerners, and translation is often more art than science. For your edification and reading pleasure, here are notes on some of the places where we could have gone in a different direction in our translation of the work, or where a Japanese cultural difference is revealed.

On Duty, page 4

Although Japanese schools hire janitors, most of the cleanup work is taken care of by the students themselves. A duty roster is made out, and two to four students are expected to stay after school (or work during other school breaks) to clean the classroom and do odd jobs necessary for the upkeep of the school.

Hatenkô Robo Dojibiron, page 8

Imadori's favorite TV program is the giant-robot show *Hatenkô Robo Dojibiron*. Hatenkô Robo means Heaven-Breaking Robot, but like the names of many other giant robots, the name of this one, Dojibiron, means nothing — it's just a combination of syllables that sounds cool to Japanese ears.

Lincoln, page 14

Yes, he said "Lincoln" in Japanese.

Duwa! and Muscle, page 18

Duwa! (and Juwa) are references to the vocalizations of the Japanese institution Ultraman. The mask with MUSCLE on it is a reference to the professional-wrestling parody manga *Kinnikuman,* which is an anime series with the tiny action figures M.U.S.C.L.E., and is seen in North America. The sequel, which also aired in the states, is called *Ultimate Muscle.*

Gokon, page 43

Gokon is a gathering of an equal number of single men and single women in a sort of speed-dating setting. (See the notes in Volume 4 for more details.)

Widdle Me, page 44
Imadori used a way of saying "teach" in Japanese that made him sound like a little child making an obvious attempt to seem cute.

MIKO-CHIN!!
CAN YOU TEACH WIDDLE ME?

Imadori Calling Her "Mikoto," page 44
Here's a perfect example of someone guilty of *yobisute*, the act of leaving off an honorific when it is highly inappropriate.

Apple Bunnies, page 47
There is a way to cut apples into quarter or eighth slices, then cut part of the peel off the wedges so that the remaining apple peel looks like rabbit ears. Very cute. But Tenma isn't skilled enough with a knife to do it.

YEAH... I WANTED TO MAKE YOU APPLE BUNNIES TO CHEER YOU ON YOUR DATE, BUT AFTER TRYING TO WORK WITH THE KNIFE, I STOPPED. BUT I KNEW THAT YOU'D BE OKAY BECAUSE YOU WERE KARERIN!
THANK GOODNESS!!
YEAH. THANKS TO YOU, IT WAS AN EASY VICTORY!
I CRUSHED IT, BUT...

Athletics Fair, page 52
These are held every year in every school. The events can take place over one or several days, and they always include races and track-and-field events. Depending on the school, the fair may also be expanded to include swimming events, team sporting events, or other Summer Olympic—style competitions. In most cases the races are between homerooms (as in this manga), but other combinations of students are possible.

Mixing English with His Japanese, page 62

In this manga, Harima said "Get out of here" and "OK" in English, while the rest of his dialog was in Japanese. Since the Japanese can read these two phrases in English and understand them, but most Westerners cannot understand the corresponding Japanese phrases, the translation left the English phrases in English.

IT IS SIMPLE.
FROM TODAY ON, YOU WILL BE MY LITTLE SISTER.
HYOOOO
OK?
HARIMA HAS A TENDENCY TO MIX ENGLISH WITH HIS JAPANESE.

Showing Your Diary, page 71

In the Japanese original, Kenji compared showing his manga pages with showing an essay to his family. In Japan, the embarrassment of showing an essay can be as great as that of showing a diary.

I COULD NEVER SHOW THEM!!
AK!
BAMM

Godfather, page 88

Yes, it was the theme to *The Godfather* in Japanese, too.

One Sôseki-san, page 94

Revered author Natsume Sôseki can be found on the Japanese thousand-yen note. So if Hanai has only one Sôseki-san, that means he has a little less than ten dollars.

Harry McKenzie, page 97

Harry McKenzie has a couple of interesting attributes. First, he looks amazingly like the character Char, the charismatic villain of the very first Gundam TV series and movies. He is also foreign, as evidenced not just by his looks and name but by his accent. He does not speak Japanese very well. This translation has tried to keep the not-quite-grammatical effect of Harry's accent in his dialogue.

Dogi, page 102

The white cotton uniform of martial artists.

Sakayaki, page 108

A samurai's *sakayaki* is the shaved part of his head where there is usually a topknot.

Lala Gonzalez, page 109

Like Harry, Lala has an accent. But since her accent is somewhat different from Harry's, this translation took a different approach for her. If her dialogue sounds just a little off to you, that's because that was intended. However, since Lala thinks in perfect Spanish (in the Japanese, her thoughts do not have the same accent indicators that her spoken Japanese does), in this book her thoughts have been translated into normal English.

Jan-ken, page 123

Jan-ken is the Japanese name for the game we know as paper-scissors-rock. The rules are the same (the Japanese play it far more than we do in the West, so be prepared for very fast play), but the name follows on a short poem spoken during the match. Players recite "*Jan-ken-pon!*" and on "*pon*," the hands are revealed. If there is a tie, the next line of the poem is, "*Aiko deshô*," which means, "Maybe it'll be another tie."

Goriyama, page 124

It seems that his name is actually Koriyama, but since Goriyama sounds somewhat like "gorilla" to Japanese ears, Goriyama is his nickname.

Second Semester, page 125

The Japanese first semester is from March or early April until July. The second semester typically begins after the six weeks of summer vacation.

Chin-Tenchô, page 129

Like *sensei*, there are many titles that can be used as honorifics. *Tenchô* is made up of the *kanji* for store and head (as in top position). The Japanese pronunciation of his name is Chin. The Mandarin Chinese pronunciations would be Chen or Zhen, and the Cantonese would be Can or Zan.

Kôhai, page 130

As referenced in the honorifics section, a *kôhai* is a younger or less experienced member of an institution, in this case, the school. *Kôhai* by one year means that since Asô is in Tenma's class and a second-year student, Sarah must be a first-year student at the same school.

Kanji in the Balloons, page 130

The customers are speaking in Chinese characters. Readers who are familiar with Japanese *kanji* will see some unfamiliar Chinese characters in the word balloons.

Kampai, page 131

Every culture has its way of making a toast with a drink, and the standard word in Japanese is *kampai*! (alternately spelled *kanpai*), pronounced "kahm-pie," and meaning "empty glass." *Kampai* is used in every situation that English speakers would use "Cheers."

Ramen Shop, page 134

When one asks a Japanese person to recommend a Chinese restaurant, most will mention the name of a good ramen shop. In a Japanese ramen shop, you will usually also find other Chinese dishes such as gyôza (pot stickers) or fried rice.

Peace Peace, page 135

The peace sign is a very common hand gesture in Japan. There are many theories about its origin, but the upshot is that whether it means peace or victory, it's a happy hand gesture in Japan.

Dainishiden, Five Tiger Generals, page 139

These references are made to fit Class 2-C's male students into the same grand scale as the Chinese epics such as *The Romance of the Three Kingdoms.* Dainishiden could be parodying chapters of the epic, changing a numbered chapter into a title that means "The Poem of Two Big Men." The Five Tiger Generals are characters who can be found in *The Romance of the Three Kingdoms.*

Three Visitations, page 140

Another slightly altered reference to *The Romance of the Three Kingdoms.* A general needed a talented ally, so he made three visitations to the potential ally's castle to beg for help. Afterward they became a powerful team. In this case, Nishimoto probably "visited" Fuyuki with three "special" videos.

Super-massive Object A, page 140

Finally! Before I went into translation, my college major was astronomy, and I can finally use that knowledge in a translation. What Osakabe-sensei is talking about is called a gravitational lens, and it does happen in the real world.

Luchador, page 145

In the Japanese, this was simply a transliteration of Luchador into Japanese characters. A Luchador is a person who performs Lucha Libre, the professional wrestling of Mexico.

Preview

We're pleased to present you a preview of Volume 6. This volume is available in English now!

《開会式!!》

…であるからして学生の本分は学業と運動の両立にあるわけであります
諸君はそれを肝に銘じていただきたい
だらだら
くどくど
2—C…おっと失礼！どこかの組のように軽挙な振る舞いでケガなどしないように！
しーーーん
…ケッ
軽挙ってなんだ？
ケガなんかするかよー
ひっこめ加藤ー
…コホン つ続いて新任の姉ケ崎妙先生をご紹介します
保健担当ですのでケガをしたら必ず診てもらうように！
ぶんぶん
みんなーー！待ってるからね〜〜〜〜〜〜!!
お姉さん、やっぱり能天気。
うおおおおお
いえーっ
っしゃあああーー!!!
思う存分ケガすんぞーー!!

★この物語はフィクションです。実在の人物、

《奈良くんの野望》
うおおお!!
美人度は2—Cがダントツだ!!
くう～～!!
俺も2—Cに入りてえ!!
奈良健太郎、青い16歳。
オツカレサマー!!
ド…ドーモ!
かっこよかったよ
つ 次は僕だ!
女子にチヤホヤされるなんて…
サ サイコーだ!
いーなあ 2—Cは
どき どき
奈良くーん♡
きゃっ!
〈奈良妄想中〉
スプーン競走
おれ あの娘 いーなー
おおー
皆 アイス買ってきたぜ———!!
ホント!?
美味しそ———!!
よし! 休憩 休憩!
どこで食べよっか?
きゃー
今鳥くんてやさしー!
ホレちゃうかもよ♡
え!?
あ…
ちょっ……!

《ララ、奮闘中!!》
しゃわ
しゃわ
しゅわ
しゅわ
ララ、意外と素直。
なんか…嫌々やってないか!?
顔怒ってねえ?
「日本では女子は皆 チアをやるのサ」って
東郷がムリヤリ…
似合ってるけどな
足長いし
……
……
じー…!
あのナ ヤリたくないならヤラなくてもいーんだゾ?
(な!?)
Real!?

《播磨、原稿執筆中》

体育祭なんてやってらんねえっスよね！
…つーか、播磨さんはなんで保健室にいるんスか？
いつもは屋上でしょ？
キィッ
え!? あ ああ！
たまにはな…
隠さないでくださいよ！
妙ちゃんが目当てでしょ？
ウヒヒヒヒ
?
体育祭なんかより妙ちゃんと話してるほーがゼッタイいいっスよ！
お目が高い！
あ ああ
そうだな…
早く消えろバカ！
↑原稿
あ 居た居た 播磨くーん！出番だよ
カラッ
!!
天満ちゃん！
悪ぃな塚本 播磨さんは出ねーぜ！
へへっ
今 俺達には体育祭になんか出ているヒマは——
この男の名前、吉田山次郎。
あるに決まってるだろーが!!
ブハ!!!

BY SATOMI IKEZAWA

WINNER OF THE KODANSHA MANGA OF THE YEAR AWARD!

Ponta is a normal Labrador retriever puppy, the Koizumi family's pet. Full of energy, she is always up to some kind of trouble. However, when Grandpa Koizumi, a passionate amateur inventor, creates the "Guru Guru Bone," which empowers animals with human speech, Ponta turns into a human girl!

Ponta dashes out into the street and is saved by Mirai Iwaki, the most popular boy at school! Her heart pounds and her face flushes. Why does she feel this way? Can there be love between a human and a dog?

The effects of the "Guru Guru Bone" are not permanent, and Ponta turns back and forth between dog and girl.

Ages: 13 +

Special extras in each volume! Read them all!

DEL REY

VISIT WWW.DELREYMANGA.COM TO:
- View release date calendars for upcoming volumes
- Sign up for Del Rey's free manga e-newsletter
- Find out the latest about new Del Rey Manga series

You're going the wrong way!

Manga is a completely different type of reading experience.

To start at the *beginning*, go to the *end*!

That's right! Authentic manga is read the traditional Japanese way—from right to left. Exactly the *opposite* of how American books are read. It's easy to follow: Just go to the other end of the book, and read each page—and each panel—from right side to left side, starting at the top right. Now you're experiencing manga as it was meant to be!